The Mental Health of Asian Americans

Contemporary Issues in Identifying and Treating Mental Problems

Stanley Sue
James K. Morishima

The Mental Health
of Asian Americans

Jossey-Bass Publishers
San Francisco • Oxford • 1990

THE MENTAL HEALTH OF ASIAN AMERICANS
Contemporary Issues in Identifying and Treating Mental Problems
by Stanley Sue and James K. Morishima

Copyright © 1982 by: Jossey-Bass Inc., Publishers
350 Sansome Street
San Francisco, California 94104
&
Jossey-Bass Limited
Headington Hill Hall
Oxford OX3 0BW

Library of Congress Cataloging in Publication Data

Sue, Stanley.
    The mental health of Asian Americans.

        Bibliography: p. 189
        Includes index.
        1. Asian Americans—Mental health. 2. Asian
Americans—Mental health services. 3. Mental
health services—United States. I. Morishima,
James K. II. Title. [DNLM: 1. Asian americans—
Psychology. 2. Mental health. 3. Mental disorders.
WA 305 S944m]
RC451.5.A75893   1982   362.2'08995073   82-48060
ISBN 0-87589-535-2

Manufactured in the United States of America

The paper in this book meets the guidelines for
permanence and durability of the Committee on
Production Guidelines for Book Longevity of the
Council on Library Resources.

JACKET DESIGN BY WILLI BAUM

FIRST EDITION
    First printing: September 1982
    Second printing: October 1985
    Third printing: May 1988
    Fourth printing: September 1990
Code 8229

The Jossey-Bass
Social and Behavioral Science Series

Preface

Several years ago we began a project funded by the National Institute of Mental Health to write an annotated bibliography of the literature on mental health of Asian and Pacific Americans. The purpose of the bibliography was to expose mental health researchers, practitioners, students, and the general public to the diverse work being conducted in the field. Having accomplished that initial task (see Morishima and others, 1979), we have written this companion volume addressed to professionals, researchers, and graduate students in the fields of psychology, psychiatry, social work, nursing, sociology, and anthropology. This book—which updates, examines, and interprets the literature and issues relevant to Asian/Pacific American mental health —grew out of our concern over the lack of systematic research and mental health programs for these minority groups. We know of no other book in the field that has comprehensively attempted to cover all the issues presented here. For this reason the task has been challenging.

The term *Asian/Pacific Americans* refers to a number of diverse groups: "(1) the descendents of immigrants from China, Japan, Korea, the Philippines, Southeast Asia (Thailand, Vietnam), East Asia (Tibet, Ryukyu Islands), and Oceania (Samoa, Guam); (2) immigrants from those areas in Asia; and (3) children of mixed marriages where one of the parents is Asian American" (Morishima, 1978, p. 8). Admittedly, the term implies a homogeneity that is lacking among these peoples and ignores the vast language and cultural differences. We have tried to do justice to these between-group differences. At the same time, the term is useful because it suggests that common issues confront all Asian/Pacific American groups. (Throughout, we refer to these groups as "Asian Americans," "Asian Americans/ Pacific Islanders," "Pacific/Asian Americans," or "Asian/Pacific Americans"; we use the terms interchangeably, reflecting designations in common use.)

In Chapter One we indicate the importance of gaining knowledge, suggesting directions for research and service delivery and developing means for implementing strategies to promote the mental health of Asian Americans. The study of Asian Americans as a visible minority group may lead to a better understanding of race relations and to improved theories and treatment strategies. We also describe the perspective adopted in this book—a perspective that stresses culture and cultural relativism, person-environment match, minority group experiences and history, and a diasthesis-stressor-resource model of mental health.

Chapter Two considers current definitions of mental disturbance and current methods of determining rates of disturbance among Asian Americans. In view of methodological and conceptual problems, we suggest that the rates of disturbance are unknown; we conclude, however, that the "untreated-case method" of determining rates should prove more fruitful than the prevalent "treated-case method." Specific symptom patterns, high-risk populations, and special mental health problems (such as drug abuse and suicide) are discussed in Chapter Three.

Chapter Four deals with family and culture. Much has been said of the importance of family and kin among Asian American groups. In this chapter we try to identify characteristics of the family and to indicate the costs and benefits of Asian American families. Particularly relevant to the discussion are the theories of Hsu (1971) and DeVos (1978) with respect to family structure. We conclude that family structure can act as a stressor or as a resource in mental health.

Issues involving personality, sex roles, and identity are presented in Chapter Five. Here we discuss the validity of Asian American stereotypes; research into personality patterns; and factors influencing personality development, sex roles, and Asian American identity. These issues have generated considerable controversy among Asian Americans—a controversy that we discuss in detail. We also examine sex role conflicts, as well as interracial marriage and its implications for ethnic identity.

In Chapter Six we discuss specific ways in which intervention and treatment can be improved. First of all, "person-environment match" can be enhanced if therapists become more knowledgeable of and sensitive to the special needs and values of Asian American clients. The "match" also can be enhanced if changes are made in the system of mental health services, so that they too are more responsive to the needs of Asian Americans. Another approach is to strengthen or build "natural" resources in the community—resources outside of the professional mental health sphere.

Chapter Seven deals with research and theory. Although research and theory are discussed throughout the book, this chapter focuses on methodological and conceptual problems encountered by researchers on Asian American personality and mental health. Suggestions for more adequate research and conceptual approaches as well as research priority areas are given.

The final chapter summarizes our main recommendations and conclusions. We also attempt to identify unresolved issues that will be particularly prominent in the future.

The book will be of value to practitioners, researchers, and graduate students. For practitioners, we provide an understanding of the clinical symptoms in psychological disturbance, the cultural and social context of such disturbance, and the means to develop effective clinical and community interventions to enhance Asian American mental health. For researchers, we have critically evaluated the existing research and theories. The evaluation implicitly suggests ways to improve methodological and conceptual approaches in Asian American research. For graduate students and others interested in Asian Americans, we hope to satisfy the need for a comprehensive and in-depth analysis of issues in Asian American mental health.

We gratefully acknowledge the assistance of various individuals who contributed to the project: Amado Cabesas, Robert Chin, Tim Dong, Lucie Cheng Hirata, Bok-Lim Kim, Sheldon Korchin, Ford Kuramoto, K. Patrick Okura, Derald Sue, and Herbert Z. Wong. We appreciate the grant support from the Center for Minority Group Mental Health Programs of the National Institute of Mental Health (Grant No. 5 RO1 MH27235).

August 1982   Stanley Sue
                                        Los Angeles, California

                                        James K. Morishima
                                        Seattle, Washington

Contents

The Authors

Stanley Sue is professor of psychology at the University of California, Los Angeles. He received his B.S. degree in psychology from the University of Oregon (1966) and his Ph.D. degree in psychology from the University of California, Los Angeles (1971). For ten years, Sue served on the Psychology faculty at the University of Washington and was director of Clinical-Community Psychology Training at the National Asian American Psychology Training Center in San Francisco in 1980-1981. He has served on the editorial boards of *American Psychologist, American Journal of Community Psychology, Journal of Community Psychology,* and *Hispanic Journal of Behavioral Sciences.* His publications have appeared in *Journal of Consulting and Clinical Psychology, American Journal of Community Psychology, Journal of Social Issues,* and *American Psychologist.* He coauthored *Understanding Abnormal Behavior* (1981) with his brothers, David Sue and Derald Sue. He is currently studying Chinese American achievements with a grant from the Rockefeller Foundation.

James K. Morishima is associate dean for graduate programs and research, College of Education, at the University of Washington. He received his B.S. and Ph.D. degrees in psychology from the

University of Washington in 1962 and 1967, respectively. An associate professor of higher education at the University of Washington from 1971 to the present, he has served as director of the Office of Institutional Educational Research (1962-1975), director of the Asian American studies program (1970-1976), and chairperson of the higher education program (1977-1982). He was vice-chairperson of an initial review group at the National Institute of Mental Health's Center for Minority Group Mental Health Programs from 1973 to 1978 and secretary for the Association of Institutional Research from 1965 to 1973. Morishima's research interests, aside from Asian American mental health, include learning styles, stress, and the organization of institutions of higher education.

The Mental Health
of Asian Americans

*Contemporary Issues in Identifying
and Treating Mental Problems*

1

Cultural Perspectives on Mental Health Issues

In 1978 the President's Commission on Mental Health urged that particular attention be paid to the needs and problems of racial and ethnic minorities, and it recommended policy changes for that purpose. Such recommendations were, for the most part, not new. Researchers, practitioners, and consumers had for many years suggested that alternate strategies be used in the development of human services or research and theory with Asian, Black, Hispanic, and Native Americans. Never before, however, had an authoritative body, such as the commission, recognized the limitations in promoting human welfare when cultural and minority group experiences are not taken into account. The commission's stance was in marked contrast to the position adopted by the Joint Commission on Mental Illness and Health (1961), which had issued an important report seven years earlier. While the joint commission found evidence that racial factors did produce stress on members of racial and ethnic minorities, it did not feel that improvement of racial conditions was in the domain of preventive psychiatry (Ewalt, 1977).

Awareness of the need for change is a motivator, necessary but not sufficient for actualization. For example, *knowledge* that racial and ethnic minorities are unserved or underserved by mental health services, are subjected to special stress conditions, and have often been misunderstood may act as a spur to alter conditions. But one still may not know what kinds of changes should occur and what intervention techniques are effective. Knowing that large segments of the population are not receiving adequate mental health care does not provide much insight into the development of better services; dissatisfaction with current research strategies does not automatically lead to improved research *directions* or to the *means* for implementing these new directions. Similarly, many training programs in clinical psychology, psychosocial nursing, social work, counseling, and psychiatry emphasize the importance of developing clinical skills in working with culturally dissimilar clients. But how can students and practitioners be better trained?

In this book we begin the task of reviewing and critically evaluating aspects of the mental health of Asian Americans and Pacific Islanders: their mental health needs and problems, delivery of services to them, and research and theories about them. Our emphasis is on *beginning* the task (rather than on *resolving* the issues) of evaluating the state of knowledge, of defining directions, and of specifying means for implementation.

Why Study Asian Americans?

Asian Americans currently make up about 2 percent of the population of the United States, and this percentage is increasing. In 1980 alone, about 40,000 immigrants came from the Philippines; 34,000 from Korea; and 5,000 from Japan; there were also 24,000 Chinese immigrants from various countries in Asia. As of 1979, more than 187,000 Indochinese refugees had been admitted since the spring of 1975; furthermore, the United States indicated its commitment to admit 25,000 Southeast Asian refugees a year over the next few years (U.S.

Comptroller General, 1979). Refugees and immigrants constitute a marked change in the composition of the Asian American population. In 1980 Asian Americans numbered about 3.5 million, with approximately 806,000 Chinese Americans; 775,000 Pilipino Americans; 701,000 Japanese Americans; 355,000 Korean Americans; 170,000 Hawaiian Americans; 270,000 "Indochinese" Americans; 42,000 Samoan Americans; 32,000 Guamanian Americans; and 400,000 others of Asian ancestry. Their population figure in 1970 was approximately 1.5 million. The rapid growth in the populations and the shifting composition of Asian Americans imply the necessity for planning in order to meet their educational, economic, and health needs.

Because those who come into contact with Asian Americans often see mainly well-educated, high-achieving, and upwardly mobile individuals, the notion that Asian Americans are victims of racism is difficult for many individuals to understand, especially since our race relations model is largely a Black-White one. That is, discrimination against Blacks is "real" because the presumed effects—such as unemployment and poverty—can be demonstrated. In our view, racial conditions also act as stressors for Asian Americans, and research and theory on the mental health of these people have often been based on faulty assumptions.

By understanding the problems and needs of Asian Americans, we may be able to gain insight into broader mental health issues. The study of culturally different groups tests the limits and generality of psychological theories and mental health practices. If traditional assumptions and theories of mental health are valid across cultures and situations, then they constitute universals. Similarly, means of conducting psychotherapy and of delivering services that are effective with a diverse range of client types indicate universal applicability. Without a culturally diverse population of study, it is difficult to determine when universals have been found or when techniques and assumptions are culturally specific—that is, applicable only to the particular cultural group in question—or universal. The importance of such a distinction is advocated by Triandis (1972), who differentiates *emic* and *etic* approaches. The emic approach describes social phenomena and utilizes concepts developed from the examination of only one culture. The etic approach emphasizes the general description of social phenomena with concepts that are universal, culture free, or pancultural. If one confuses emic with etic concepts, then theories and practices may be inappropriately applied across cultures. Such confusion can have disastrous results, as the following article from the *Seattle Times* (April 19, 1979) illustrates:

> The Cook County public guardian, Patrick T. Murphy, filed a $5 million suit yesterday against the Illinois director of mental health and his predecessors, charging that they kept a Chinese immigrant in custody for twenty-seven years mainly because the man could not speak English. The federal court suit charged that the Illinois Department of Mental Health had never treated the patient, identified only as David T., for any mental disorders and had found a Chinese-speaking psychologist to talk to him only after twenty-five years. The suit said that David, who is in his fifties, was put in Oak Forest Hospital, then known as Oak Forest Tuberculosis Hospital, in 1952. He was transferred to a state mental hospital where doctors conceded they could not give him a mental exam because he spoke little English. But they diagnosed him as psychotic anyway. The suit said that in 1971 a doctor who spoke no Chinese said David answered questions in an "incoherent and unintelligible manner." It was charged also that David was quiet and caused little trouble but was placed in restraints sometimes because he would wander to a nearby ward that housed the only other Chinese-speaking patient.

It is unclear how common such situations are, although in California a similar case was also reported. The point is that people should not disregard cultural differences, which influence assessment procedures, treatment approaches, research methodologies, and theories.

The mental health issues and concerns of Asian Americans are clearly described in a task force report to the President's Commission on Mental Health. The report (see President's Commission on Mental Health, 1978, vol. 3) contains sixty-seven recommendations covering the areas of social policies, delivery of mental health services, training and personnel, research, and prevention. The task force expressed concern over the cultural responsiveness of treatment and therapy, the plight of immigrants and refugees, the lack of Asian American representation in policy-making roles, the need for community participation in mental health, the training of competent mental health workers, and the adequacy of current research. In a sense, the report indicated "what is" (the current status of Asian American mental health) and "what should be" (the recommendations). Since the interest of this book is on current knowledge of Asian American mental health, directions for the future, and the means of implementation, we shall refer to the report throughout the book.

Our Conceptual Framework

Our goal is to review and critically examine Asian American mental health research and to suggest directions for research, intervention, and training. Certain values or viewpoints serve as our general conceptual framework. The constituent parts of this framework are described in the following sections.

Culture and Cultural Relativism. Kluckhohn and Murray (1956) observed that every person is in certain respects like all other persons, like some but not all other persons, and like no other person. One can choose to emphasize commonalities or individual differences among human beings. When we speak of a group's culture, we are referring to certain shared experiences that result in typical ways of perceiving, interpreting, and behaving. A more precise definition of culture is problematic. Kroeber and Kluckhohn (1952) reviewed over 150 definitions and concluded: "Culture consists of patterns, explicit and implicit, of and for behavior acquired and transmitted by symbols, constituting the distinctive achievement of human groups, including their embodiments in artifacts; the essential core of culture consists of traditional (that is, historically derived and selected) ideas and especially their attached values; culture systems may on the one hand be considered as products of action, on the other as conditioning elements of further action" (p. 180). They acknowledge that culture can be considered as an outcome or as a cause of action. We are interested primarily in culture as a cause—specifically, in the influence of culture on the perceptions, interpretations, and behaviors of persons in a specific culture. Thus, issues such as cultural differences in defining mental health, social supports, and utilization of mental health services are important to us. These issues should be viewed from a relative position in which cultural specific rather than universal aspects are appreciated. Research strategies are also implicated in these issues, since it is through research that cultural differences can be determined. Strategies themselves may be culturally biased and inappropriate across different cultures.

Given that cultures often differ, what is the best way to conceptualize these differences? How can individual differences within culture be appropriately represented? If cultures substantially overlap in most characteristics, when do cultural differences really make a difference? Many investigators adopt the concept of a modal personality. That is, cultures may differ in the average scores on any particular attribute (Inkeles and Levinson, 1969). The greater the difference, the more meaningful the attribute in differentiating cultures. To say that Pilipino Americans rely heavily on the extended family for support does not imply that Westerners or Caucasian Americans lack this characteristic or resource. Instead, the statement suggests that the groups have modal differences that are important to consider. Similarly, in view of within-group variability, it is not expected that all persons within a given culture will possess the characteristics associated with a modal personality description. In other words, we will try to indicate important cultural factors affecting Asian American mental health while acknowledging similarities and differences both between and within groups.

Person-Environment Match. Another theme of this book, and one that has implications for conceptualizing Asian American experiences as well as implementing courses of action, is the importance of the person-environment fit. Rappaport (1977) has taken the position that there are neither inadequate persons nor inadequate environments; rather, the fit or match between persons and environments may be in relative accord or discord. The implications of this position are that (1) increasing the match or fit is important, (2) looking for weaknesses of people and communities is less important than creating alternatives that utilize and develop existing strengths and resources, and (3) differences among people and communities may be desirable. Traditionally, ethnic minority groups in general and Asian Americans in particular have been caught between two positions. The first is the assimilation model, where minority group cultures are expected to adopt majority or mainstream values and behavioral patterns. The assumption is that minority group cultures fail to transmit functional skills that members need in order to succeed in the dominant society; therefore, American styles of personality and social interaction should replace previous patterns learned in Asian cultures. The second is the pluralism model, which suggests that ethnic minority cultures have strengths and should be encouraged. According to this model, functional skills are necessary, but total assimilation is not desirable; in fact, if ethnic patterns were extinguished, identity conflicts and emotional problems would result. Neither of these models recognizes simultaneous change in persons and environments. In mental health and the delivery of mental health services, the person-environment match through simultaneous changes should be of paramount concern.

Minority Group Experiences and History. Social scientists often limit their discussion of Asians in the United States to cultural factors. Asian Americans are perceived to be culturally different from those in the mainstream culture. Therefore, to understand and enhance psychotherapy approaches, the emphasis is on responding to cultural differences. Indeed, a number of current books and articles deal with cross-cultural therapy (see Pedersen, Lonner, and Draguns, 1976). However, scholars and practitioners need to do more than simply understand various Asian and Asian American cultures. The well-being of Asian Americans is not just a matter of reducing cultural conflicts, of having culturally responsive services, or of understanding Asian

American cultural values. For well over a century, Asian Americans and the larger American society have evolved patterns of interactions, values, stereotypes, and practices. It would be difficult to characterize Black and White Americans as simply having cultural differences. Rather, patterns of racism, prejudice, and discrimination are intimately involved in Black-White relationships and help to explain racial differences in perceptions, values, and behaviors. Asian American-White experiences are also important to recognize. Cultural differences and minority group experiences must be jointly examined if one is to fully understand Asian Americans. The reluctance of Asian Americans to utilize mental health services may be due to different cultural values or attitudes toward mental health or toward services. Another plausible explanation for this phenomenon is that some Asian Americans, experiencing racial prejudice or discrimination, may avoid services because of distrust or suspiciousness. Minority group experiences do affect mental health.

The designation of Asian Americans as a minority group that has experienced prejudice and discrimination is misunderstood by many persons. The misunderstanding is based largely on the failure to accurately assess the status of Asian Americans and to conceptualize racial discrimination. Popular notions of discrimination are grounded in Black-White race relationships. Racism against Blacks is apparent because of the history of exploitation and the presumed consequences in social, economic, occupational, educational, and health indicators. While historians and others familiar with Asian Americans readily agree that Asian Americans have had a history of exploitation and racism in the United States (Lyman, 1974), many persons argue that, unlike Blacks, Asian Americans have high upward mobility in education, income, and occupation. How can Asian Americans be regarded as an oppressed minority group? This question, debated over the past ten years, is an important one with mental health implications. If Asian Americans encounter racism, then they experience a significant stressor, and enhancement of mental health would include the elimination of this stressor, the encompassing of Asian Americans in affirmative action programs, and the analysis of mental health systems as products of a racist society. It would also be instructive to determine how various individuals have been able to adjust to these conditions. On the other hand, if discrimination and prejudice are historical rather than contemporary in nature, then the important questions are: What factors have caused the change for Asian Americans, and why are there persistent claims from Asian Americans that they are the victims of discrimination? Asian Americans still experience stereotyping, prejudicial attitudes, and discrimination. These experiences affect psychological well-being, as discussed in subsequent chapters.

In one sense, the debate over the status of Asian Americans has been a healthy one. It has challenged traditional assumptions about their success and has led to more sensitive research. One cannot but be impressed by the geometric increase in research on Asian Americans within the past decade. Four perspectives have emerged: the model minority image, the high-risk orientation, the oppressed image, and the self-interest orientation.

The *model minority image* of Asian Americans has been the most persistent and popular. In this view, Asian Americans are extremely upwardly mobile—as evidenced by such cultural traits as industriousness, discipline, thriftiness, and willingness to sacrifice. Not only are Asian Americans well accepted in American society but they also have very "positive" stereotypes and are well regarded. In view of their extraordinary achievements, there is no need to include them in affirmative action or special programs for minority groups.

The *high-risk orientation* implicitly acknowledges that some Asian Americans have fared well in society. The concern is over certain groups that are particularly vulnerable to problems. These groups include immigrants, refugees, Chinatown youths, the elderly, and other disadvantaged segments who are under increased stress. Emerging Asian American groups such as Pilipino and Vietnamese Americans or Pacific Islander Americans such as the Samoan Americans are also considered high risk in that their history in the United States is shorter and their social indicators of well-being are not as high as those for Chinese and Japanese Americans. The task is to select those groups that need special attention and resources.

The *oppressed image* of Asian Americans casts them

victims of racism. Statistics on their well-being tend to be misleading and often ignore the major problems that they encounter as a result of prejudice and discrimination. Some groups (such as immigrants or the elderly) are particularly powerless; nevertheless, Asian Americans as a whole experience the same institutional conditions that Blacks, Hispanics, and Native Americans face. If racism affects mental health, then Asian Americans have this additional stressor and pay its price. If racism affects mental health services, then Asian Americans are likely to receive unresponsive services. The oppressed image would suggest improved research strategies, free from biases and stereotypes, that assess the mental health of Asian Americans and modifications in the service delivery system. The underlying process is to eliminate racism in order to foster mental health.

The *self-interest orientation* is concerned with the status of Asian Americans. It matters little if Asian Americans are successful or unsuccessful. Regardless of their current well-being, the goal is to constantly monitor, advocate, and implement policies that serve Asian American interests. The philosophy is not unlike those of labor unions, corporations, or other special-interest groups. There is no need to document problems of Asian Americans unless it is an effective way of drawing attention and resources to this group. If Asian Americans are doing well, the goal is to maintain high status or to enhance it. Political influence, lobbying, and exertion of power are the concrete means of trying to protect the interests of Asian Americans, a minority group.

These four perspectives are important in mental health policy and in defining group identity. They also provoke intense controversy and have been debated in much of the Asian American literature (Morishima and others, 1979; Sue, Sue, and Sue, 1975).

Diathesis-Stressor-Resource. If asked what causes mental disturbance, most mental health professionals would generally agree on a diathesis-stress conceptualization, where constitutional factors (such as heredity and physiological variables) and life experiences (such as broken homes, childhood traumas, or exposure to noxious stimuli) interact to create mental disturbance. However, given the same constitutional makeup and exposed to similar life stressors, individuals often respond quite differently. Some people handle stress, while others deteriorate. What determines this differential risk among people who have similar experiences? Possibly some individuals have better personal, interpersonal, and social support resources to use in times of stress. There may be, then, a need for a diathesis-stressor-resource model of psychopathology. Presumably, individuals who have physiological abnormalities or weaknesses, encounter severe stress, and have few resources with which to cope are vulnerable to mental disturbance.

While constitutional factors are undoubtedly important, we know little about racial differences in these factors (except in expressions of symptom patterns and in possible psychological reactions to drugs and alcohol). In order to understand Asian American mental health, we must analyze the stressors and resources that are conditioned by history and culture. Individuals can be positioned on two dimensions: (1) the presence or absence of significant stressors and (2) the presence or absence of significant resources. Stressors can vary in intensity, duration, and number, while resources can vary in availability, number, and quality. The task is to specify those stressors and resources that may be relevant to Asian Americans.

The primary stressors discussed in this book are culture conflict, minority group status, and social change. The resources are professional mental health services and natural support systems (such as families, kin, friends, working associates, and clubs). For Kelly (1977), social supports represent acts and deeds that help persons (1) master their environment, (2) retain or increase their self-esteem in their social milieus, and (3) participate actively in their communities. Caplan (1972) feels that support systems enable individuals to maintain themselves in relative health and comfort. Natural support systems are, then, the main resources in promoting mental health.

What kinds of natural support systems are available to Asian Americans? History and culture appear to be key factors in determining the nature of support systems. Because of their history in the United States, various Asian American groups have had to develop their unique patterns of social supports. Cultural factors also determine the evolution or maintenance of social support systems. The extended family and kinship system often provides assistance for Asian Americans (Ponce, 1977). Chin (1982) identifies third-party intermediaries that act as resources among Chinese Americans. It is clear that in order to conceptualize Asian American mental health, knowledge about culturally and historically determined support systems must be gained.

2

Patterns of Disturbance and Use of Services

The behavior of Japanese Americans has, in some instances, gone directly counter to many sociological hypotheses concerning the negative force of discrimination in American society. By and large they have succeeded relatively well in American society, despite the history of strong prejudice against them. . . . This is witnessed in social statistics in a relative lack of delinquency in youth, and a relative lack of observable mental illness, at least as indicated by mental hospital statistics [DeVos, 1978, p. 4].

Previously we referred to a study indicating the prevalence of alcoholism among Caucasian Americans in Hawaii and the lack of it among their fellow islanders, the former Chinese nationals and their offspring. From the same source we learn that the incidence of mental illness per one hundred thousand persons is highest among the Whites and lowest among the Chinese. Significantly, the rate of mental illness which was of organic origin was nearly constant for all racial groups [Hsu, 1970, p. 68].

It is disturbing to note that many Americans still believe that Asian Americans (1) experience few mental health problems, (2) have little need for mental health related social services, and (3) have sufficient resources, manpower, and otherwise, for those with such needs. The evidence is convincingly contrary. The unmet mental health needs and gaps in services are substantial. These needs will be considerably multiplied with the known steady increase in the Asian American population in the United States [testimony from Herbert Z. Wong before the President's Commission on Mental Health, March 1977].

In comparing these three statements, one might be tempted to conclude that Wong's position covers all Asian Americans whereas the comments of DeVos and Hsu are relevant to Japanese and Chinese Americans, respectively; thus, Wong's deep concern over the mental health of Asian Americans need not contradict the positive statements by DeVos and Hsu. This, however, is not the case. Substantial disagreements exist over the psychological well-being of all Asian Americans (Sue, Sue, and Sue, 1975). Which view is correct? Are Asian Americans relatively well adjusted and mentally healthy, or do they have substantial mental health problems? Which position is best supported by the available research findings? Is the available research an accurate indicator of Asian American mental health? In this chapter we examine rates of mental disturbance among Asian Americans. The methodology and conceptual problems of research in this area are noted.

Definitions of Mental Disturbance

In his classic paper on research criteria for mental disturbance, Scott (1958) identified six operational definitions of disturbance:

1. *Mental Disturbance as Exposure to Mental Health*

Treatment. The most frequently used operational definition of mental disturbance is the fact that a person receives treatment. Records from mental hospitals, outpatient clinics, and private practitioners may be obtained to ascertain the demand for mental health treatment. The major advantages in this definition are simplicity and the availability of data. That is, patient records are routinely collected by most practitioners, so that it is a relatively easy matter to determine what kinds of persons seek services for mental health problems. The definition is operational rather than conceptual, since no attempt is made to understand the nature of mental disturbance. Some persons may be treated when, in fact, they are not mentally disturbed. For example, friends or relatives of a person may inappropriately recommend that the person undergo treatment when the person really does not have emotional problems. The most serious difficulty with the "exposure to treatment" definition is that it fails to identify mentally disturbed persons who do not seek mental health services—who, for one reason or another, do not enter the professional mental health system. Thus, the definition undercounts the number of persons needing (as opposed to receiving) services. This undercounting would not be a serious problem if one could, on the basis of those exposed to treatment, (1) reasonably project rates of mental disturbance to the entire population and (2) be assured that systematic biases do not exist in the utilization of mental health services for various groups in the population. However, these two tasks cannot be fulfilled in practice.

2. *Social Maladjustment as a Definition of Disturbance.* Deviation from social norms, group standards, or even laws may be used in the definition of mental disturbance. A social group, a community, or the broader society may provide a consensus on appropriate behaviors; and behaviors discordant with the consensus or norm may be taken as evidence of psychopathology. While such a definition often appeals to cultural relativists, who feel that individual groups should determine what constitutes good and poor adjustment, it has major disadvantages. Community consensus may be lacking, and specification of the adjustment criteria and of the frame of reference (the issue of whose standards are being applied) complicates matters. In our

discussion of Asian Americans, we do not extensively examine this definition except to acknowledge that different groups often define mental health and disturbance according to their own cultural values.

3. *Psychiatric Diagnosis as a Definition of Disturbance.* The advantage of using psychiatric diagnosis is that particular kinds of mental disorders can be specified and compared across different groups in the population. For example, one may be interested in the relative proportions of psychotic versus nonpsychotic disorders among different races or social classes. Or one might study the influence of cultural backgrounds on symptom patterns of persons who are culturally dissimilar but who have the same psychiatric diagnosis, such as schizophrenia. The utility of psychiatric diagnosis depends on (1) the reliability and validity of the diagnostic system and the accuracy of the diagnostician and (2) the ability to generalize from diagnosed samples to the population. If the samples are biased, then the relative proportions of disorders in the population and the ability to compare disorders across different cultures may be affected. In our discussion we shall refer to broad categories (for example, psychotic) rather than narrow ones (such as paranoid schizophrenia or disorganized schizophrenia), since the broader the category, the more reliable the diagnosis (Korchin, 1976).

4. *Subjective Report as a Definition of Mental Disturbance.* Subjective reports of distress, disturbance, depression, or anxiety may serve as criteria for mental disturbance. While intuitively appealing as a definition of emotional disturbance, subjective reports depend on the ability and willingness of persons to self-disclose. Antisocial personalities or psychopaths may not be upset by their own behaviors, and certain individuals report feelings of anxiety but function well in social and occupational areas. Furthermore, unhappiness may be largely due to situational factors, so that the disturbance felt by some persons may not be caused by some underlying personality pattern but rather by a person-environment mismatch. We know of no Asian American studies that investigate subjective reports of distress (not counting personality testing).

5. *Presence of Symptoms as a Definition of Mental Dis-*

turbance. Another criterion of mental disturbance involves the presence of symptoms as revealed through "objective" personality inventories or measures that have been validated against an accepted criterion. For example, the investigators who developed the Minnesota Multiphasic Personality Inventory (MMPI) used an empirical procedure to determine item and scale patterns that could discriminate between normal and psychiatric groups. If subjects obtain certain scores on personality inventories, they are judged to have characteristics found in psychiatric populations. Objective personality tests are widely used and have been extremely valuable in the mental health field. In cross-cultural research, however, the utility of the measures is limited because the tests may not have been empirically validated across cultures and because different cultures may have different response sets. In their study of *normal* (nonpatient) Puerto Rican and Black Americans, Dohrenwend and Dohrenwend (1969) found that the Puerto Ricans received higher test scores for psychological disorders than the Blacks, suggesting that Puerto Rican Americans have more psychological disturbance. When the same test was administered to Puerto Rican and Black American *patient* groups, matched on types of disorders, Puerto Rican Americans again had higher scores. Why should Puerto Rican American patients have higher scores than Black American patients who were matched on the types of disorders? The Dohrenwends believe that Puerto Rican Americans may be more likely to endorse items indicative of psychological disturbance. That is, the response differences may be due to cultural modes of symptom expression rather than to actual differences in underlying psychological disorders. Differences between Asian and Caucasian Americans in objective personality inventory scores are often difficult to interpret in view of possible response sets.

6. *Positive Mental Health as a Criterion.* While the five previous definitions of mental disturbance primarily stress the presence of symptoms and problems or their indicators, the positive mental health perspective uses the absence of positive adaptation as the criterion. According to this definition, persons who cannot cope, who lack an adequate degree of environmental mastery, or who have deficiencies in perceiving self and

the environment are mentally unhealthy. Thus, psychological well-being is not simply a matter of being free of mental disturbance (Jahoda, 1958); if persons also fail to live up to their potentials, they may be in poor psychological health. Just as individuals may be free of disease or injury but be in poor physical health because of poor diet or the lack of exercise, persons may be free of mental disorders but have low self-esteem and little actualization of potentials.

Bradburn's (1970) research appears relevant to our discussion of positive mental health. He was interested in subjective reports of happiness and their correlates. In a survey of over 2,500 persons, happiness was inversely related to age and directly related to education and income, which are not surprising findings. Bradburn then asked respondents whether they had experienced positive and/or negative feelings over the past two weeks. Interestingly, these two components of well-being were not related to each other. Each did correlate with self-reported happiness, with positive feelings directly related, and with negative feelings inversely related, to happiness. Moreover, the difference between positive and negative affects was highly associated with self-reported happiness. Bradburn speculates that psychological well-being is not simply a matter of the absence of disturbance. Some individuals are mentally disturbed (conceptually, this situation occurs when negative affect is greater than positive affect). Others are mentally healthy (when positive affect is greater than negative affect). But there is also the third possibility of "not healthy" where positive and negative affects are equal. While positive mental health notions are often vague and poorly defined, it does seem to make sense to differentiate three categories: "sick," "well," and "not healthy." As argued by Sue (1977b), minority group experiences may affect Asian Americans not so much in increasing mental disorders as in decreasing positive mental health.

We have presented these six research definitions of mental disturbance as a means of indicating that methodological and conceptual problems become particularly acute when rates of mental disturbance in dissimilar ethnic groups are compared. This is apparent when psychiatric treatment and psychological symptoms of Asian and Caucasian Americans are compared. Indeed, the contrasting views of Asian American mental health cited earlier reflect some of the obstacles to adequately defining mental disturbance and to devising appropriate measurements.

These six research definitions of mental disturbance provide clues to the means of assessing psychological well-being. The six approaches are obviously not mutually exclusive. For example, by examining hospital records, one may simultaneously collect information on the kinds of persons receiving treatment as well as on the psychiatric diagnosis given. Patients also are often given objective personality tests.

In practice two broad epidemiological approaches are used to determine the rate and distribution of psychopathology. The first is the use of "treated" cases (exposure to psychiatric treatment), and the second is the use of "untreated" cases (self-reports of distress or psychological symptoms) obtained from surveys. We shall examine each approach, since both have been used with Asian American groups.

Treated-Case Method of Determining Rates of Disturbance

If the exposure-to-treatment definition of mental disturbance is adopted, then Asian American groups show extremely low rates of psychopathology. Kitano (1969) presented findings on the admission of patients to California state mental hospitals, based on statistics from the state's Department of Mental Hygiene. As indicated in Table 1, admission rates for mental disturbance were many times lower for Japanese and Chinese Americans than for Caucasian Americans during each of the years from 1960 to 1965. Among the other ethnic groups considered, Mexican Americans had lower rates of psychopathology than Caucasians, whereas Black Americans had higher rates. Native Americans had lower rates than Caucasians from 1961 through 1963 and equal rates during the other years.

Data from the state of Hawaii also indicate low Asian American rates of admission to state hospitals for mental disorders. Table 2 shows the ethnic distribution of patients and of the state's population. Chinese, Hawaiian, Japanese, and Pili-

Table 1. Admissions of Patients by Ethnic Groups—California State Hospitals for the Mentally Ill, 1960-1965.

Year	Japanese	Caucasian	Mexican American	Indian	Chinese	Negro
1960	40	150	40	150	70	190
1961	50	160	20	90	80	200
1962	50	170	30	140	90	210
1963	50	170	30	130	80	240
1964	60	170	40	170	90	250
1965	60	180	40	180	90	280

Group (rates per 100,000)

Note: Population base rates for each ethnic group are computed on 1960 population, United States Bureau of Census. Therefore, rates for the last several years are probably much lower for all groups.

Source: Kitano (1969).

Table 2. Admissions to Hawaii State Hospitals and
Population by Ethnicity.

Group	First Admissions (1969-1970)		Population 1970	
	Percent	Number	Percent	Number
Caucasian	48.5	346	39.2	301,429
Japanese	15.0	107	28.3	217,669
Pilipino	8.0	57	12.4	95,354
Hawaiian	.6	4	9.3	71,274
Chinese	1.5	11	6.8	52,375
Korean	—	—	1.3	9,625
Black	—	—	1.0	7,517
Indian	—	—	.2	1,216
Other	26.4	189	1.6	12,100
Total	100	714	100	768,559

Source: Based on information from State of Hawaii (1970, 1978). Hospital data for Korean, Black, and Indian groups were not available.

pino Americans all exhibited lower rates of admissions than expected from their proportions in the population.

These and other studies (Brown and others, 1973; Sue and Sue, 1974; Sue and McKinney, 1975) reveal lower rates of mental disturbance for Asian Americans than for Caucasian Americans. The consistency of the findings, however, must be weighed with some inconsistent phenomena. First, in the Kitano study, Mexican Americans had lower rates of admissions than Caucasians. If, however, as Padilla, Ruiz, and Alvarez (1975) argue, Mexican Americans are under a great deal of stress because of socioeconomic and minority group status, one would expect this group to have the same rate of mental disturbance as Caucasians, or even higher. Second, Berk and Hirata (1973) have shown that if the exposure-to-treatment definition is strictly adhered to, then rates of disturbance have increased for Chinese Americans. From 1855 to 1955, admissions to state mental hospitals in California doubled for the general population and increased over sevenfold for Chinese Americans.

Our believe is that exposure to treatment is a poor means of ascertaining the degree of mental disturbance in Asian American populations. Continued use of this strategy is misleading and perpetuates the popular notion that Asian Americans have extraordinary low rates of disturbance. We feel that at the present time it is not possible to estimate the true rates of mental disturbance. The use of treated cases underestimates the degree of psychopathology in Asian American populations because Asian Americans are more reluctant to use mental health services than are Caucasian Americans. To better understand how this is possible, let us examine three studies in greater depth. All three studies assume that Asian Americans (1) underutilize mental health facilities and (2) show greater severity of mental disturbance than Caucasian Americans do.

The first study, by Sue and Sue (1974), was stimulated by their belief that very few Chinese and Japanese American students utilized the student psychiatric clinic at the University of California, Los Angeles. In order to study the utilization patterns of these students, Sue and Sue examined the files of all students seen at the psychiatric clinic over a one-year period. Information was obtained on the number of Asian American student clients, MMPI test scores, and therapists' impressions of these clients. Findings indicated that Asian American students, representing 8 percent of the campus population, comprised only 4 percent of the clients at the psychiatric clinic. Thus, they were underrepresented by half. Since MMPI records were available, it was possible to see whether Asian American students exhibited more severe disturbances than other students. The investigators assessed severity of disturbance by comparing Asian Americans with non-Asian Americans in mean differences on MMPI scales and in the proportion of psychotic profiles as calculated from the Goldberg Formula. Results revealed that Chinese and Japanese American males and females scored higher on MMPI scales and had more psychotic profiles than their non-Asian American counterparts.

The findings supported the hypothesis that Asian Americans underutilized mental health services and exhibit greater disturbance among the client population. The suggestion is that moderately disturbed Asian Americans, unlike Caucasian Americans, are more likely to avoid using services (unless one takes the unusual and unsupported position that Asian Americans have low rates of overall disturbance but high rates of severe mental disorders). One potential problem with the study is that the use of the MMPI to compare Asian and Caucasian Americans may be inappropriate. Norms on the MMPI do not exist for Asian Americans, and the possibility of ethnic differences in response sets is real. The next two studies, however, support the findings from the MMPI, which argue against the notion that the particular findings are biased in some way.

Brown and associates (1973) conducted a study of Chinese American patients at Resthaven Community Mental Health Center, which serves the downtown Los Angeles area, including Chinatown. They examined twenty-three mental health files of the Chinese American patients at Resthaven and formed a control group of twenty-three Caucasian American patients who were matched on variables such as sex, age, financial status, and legal status (voluntary or involuntary admission). Data were obtained from patients' backgrounds, treatment records, and behavioral measures. Results indicated that the Chinese American patients were largely male (70 percent), born in China (83 percent), and Chinese speaking. Comparing the symptomology between the two groups at the time of admission yielded some interesting findings. First, on the Twelve Psychotic Syndromes of psychiatric behavior (Lorr and Vestre, 1968), Chinese Americans were significantly higher than Caucasian Americans on retardation, seclusiveness, help needed, and psychotic disorganization. Second, no racial differences were found in psychiatric diagnosis. On one measure, then, and not on the other, there was evidence of greater psychological disturbance on the part of Chinese Americans. This measure (the Twelve Psychotic Syndromes) was used to rate patients on certain behavioral patterns as judged by two raters reading case materials of patients at the time of admission and during the following ten days. The mean interrater reliability coefficient across the twelve dimensions was 0.88. Brown and his colleagues also noted that this measure has been used in cross-cultural research. They found that Chinese Americans underutilized the community mental health center by about half their expected rate on the basis of their populations in downtown Los Angeles.

In the Sue and Sue (1974) study of Asian and Caucasian American college students, demographic variables between the two groups were not controlled. Brown and his colleagues (1973) did match Chinese and Caucasian American patients on demographic variables, but their findings were limited to a single Asian American group—Chinese Americans. Both studies were conducted in a single setting. A third study, the Seattle Project conducted by Sue and McKinney (1975), included all Asian American groups, such as Chinese, Japanese, Korean, and Pilipino Americans, and dealt with seventeen community mental health centers in the greater Seattle area. By examining the records of all patients seen for a three-year period, the investigators could study utilization rates, severity of disorders, and demographic characteristics. Asian Americans were found to be many times underrepresented as patients. While they represented about 2.4 percent of the population served by the centers, only 100 (or 0.7 percent) of the 13,198 patients were Asian Americans. To determine whether they were more severely disturbed than Caucasian Americans, comparisons were made between the two groups in the proportion of functional psychotic diagnoses. For Asian American patients, 22 percent were diagnosed as psychotic, while 13 percent of the Caucasian American patients were given this diagnosis, a significant difference. Since there were racial differences in age and educational levels, these two demographic variables were controlled. Results again supported the higher proportion of psychotic diagnosis among Asian American patients.

There is convergent evidence, then, that few Asian Americans enter the professional mental health system as clients. Five studies (Kitano, 1969; State of Hawaii, 1970; Sue and Sue, 1974; Brown and others, 1973; Sue and McKinney, 1975) are consistent in their findings of underutilization. This occurs whether or not (1) Chinese, Japanese, or all Asian American groups are examined; (2) inpatient or outpatient facilities are studied; (3) students or adults are the patients; and (4) the study is limited to a single facility or a number of different mental health facilities. Furthermore, the three studies (Sue and Sue, 1974; Brown and others, 1973; Sue and McKinney, 1975) that specifically examined the severity of disorders revealed that Asian Americans have greater disturbance than the other patients, as indicated in Table 3. The measures used to assess severity were quite different, ranging from a personality inventory (MMPI) and ratings on a behavioral scale (the Twelve Psychotic Syndrome Scale) to formal psychiatric diagnosis (made presumably from clinical assessment procedures). In contrast to the findings of Sue and McKinney, Brown and his colleagues did not find diagnostic differences between Chinese and Caucasian American patients. However, they studied inpatients, who are usually quite disturbed, so that a "ceiling effect" may be operating. Their study also involved only twenty-three patients in each group, quite a small number for an analysis of diagnostic differences. Finally, it should be mentioned that the Seattle and UCLA studies looked at the prevalence of disorder (new and existing cases for the specified time interval) while Brown's Resthaven study focused on the incidence of disorders (that is, new cases for the time interval).

We believe that the most parsimonious explanation for the low rate of exposure to treatment for Asian Americans is that they are less likely than Caucasian Americans to seek mental health services for emotional problems. The traditional explanation that low utilization of services is caused by the low rate of mental disturbance is weakened by findings that Asian Americans who do seek treatment are more severely disturbed than are Caucasian Americans. This suggests that more moderately disturbed Asian Americans may simply *not* be using professional mental health services. If it can be demonstrated that Asian Americans are more reluctant to use services than Caucasian Americans are, then exposure to treatment should be viewed more as one form of help-seeking behavior than as a definition for mental disturbance.

The use of treated cases as a measure of the rate of psychopathology has frequently been criticized (Dohrenwend and Dohrenwend, 1974a). We have dwelled on this method because (1) it is still the most widely used procedure to ascertain rates, (2) the underutilization of services is still used to justify the belief that Asian Americans have exceedingly low rates of mental

Table 3. Studies of Underutilization and Severity.

	Setting	Ethnicity	Strategy	Measures	Results
Sue and Sue (1974) Los Angeles	Campus psychiatric clinic	Chinese, Japanese, and Koreans	Comparison with randomly selected non-Asian control group	MMPI	Underutilization Greater severity of disorders
Brown and others (1973) Los Angeles	Inpatient community mental health center	Chinese	Comparison with matched control of Caucasians	Behavioral ratings on psychotic syndromes	Underutilization Greater severity of disorders
Sue and McKinney (1975) Seattle	Seventeen community mental health centers	All Asian Americans	Comparison with randomly selected Caucasian group. Controls for demographic differences through statistical means	Formal psychiatric diagnosis	Underutilization Greater severity of disorders

disturbance, and (3) utilization rather than need for services usually determines program policies and directions. Thus, underutilization results not only in misunderstandings of Asian American mental health needs but also in service programs that deemphasize the delivery of services to this group.

Reasons for Underutilization of Services

In their analysis of factors that inhibit self-referrals for mental health services on the part of Chinese Americans, Tsai, Teng, and Sue (1980) list seven explanations that may be applicable to Asian Americans as a whole. These include feelings of stigma and shame over mental disturbance, availability of alternative resources, cost of mental health services, location and knowledge of service facilities, hours of operation, belief systems about mental health, and responsiveness of services.

Stigma and Shame. That mental patients are the victims of prejudice and social ostracism is well documented. In its *Report to the President,* the President's Commission on Mental Health (1978) indicated that the general public is frightened and repelled by the notion of mental disturbance and that afflicted individuals often feel too ashamed or embarrassed to seek or receive help. A number of investigators (Callao, 1973; Kitano, 1969; Tsai, Teng, and Sue, 1980) believe that Asian American groups are very reluctant to seek mental health services because of cultural values regarding the avoidance of shame and the importance of family integrity. Such behavior would be an admission of personal weakness and "bad blood" and would bring disgrace on both the seekers and their families. As noted by Ponce (1974, p. 42), "The Filipino is likely to view the mental health worker with alarm or confusion—alarm because the presence of the mental health worker may reinforce a belief that he is insane or weak, and confusion because he honestly may not understand why he should be seeing the mental health worker. From the very start, the mental health worker is under a heavy handicap." *Haji* for the Japanese, *hiya* for the Pilipino, *mentz* for the Chinese, and *chaemyun* for the Korean Americans are terms used to convey feelings involving embarrassment, shame, and loss of face (Kim, 1978). Cultural values among Asian Americans may inhibit self-referral for mental health services, and the inhibition may be stronger among those in Asian than in Western cultures.

Sue and Kirk (1975) compared the utilization of counseling and psychiatric services by Chinese and Japanese American students at the University of California, Berkeley. It was their impression that relative to others the Asian American students tended to overutilize counseling services and to underutilize psychiatric services—perhaps because counseling services provided a broader range of assistance (personal, academic, vocational) than psychiatric services and operated with less stigma and threat to one's mental health status. The results of the study confirmed their hypothesis. Asian American students were more likely to seek help from the counseling center than were other students, who, in turn, utilized the psychiatric services more than Asian Americans did. Stigma and shame may indeed inhibit the utilization of services strongly identified as psychiatric or mental health in nature.

Morishima (1975), noting that one private mental health practitioner had eighteen active Asian American clients, speculates that middle-class Asian Americans may seek out private care, rather than public or quasi-public mental health facilities. He suggests that studies measuring utilization rates should be conducted among public, quasi-public, private, and traditional mental health providers. Further, he suggests that many Asian Americans may exhibit psychological distress in psychophysiological complaints and, consequently, seek out medical practitioners rather than mental health professionals.

Availability of Alternative Resources. Another explanation for the underutilization of services is that some Asian Americans may have alternate resources to deal with emotional problems—resources that are culturally consistent with their life-style. In a study of help-seeking behavior among Chinese Canadians in Vancouver, British Columbia, Lin and his associates (1978) found that many families tended to assist and intervene in the problems of particular individuals. There was great tolerance of serious psychotic symptoms as long as excessively disruptive behaviors were not present. When extrafamilial sources of assistance were sought, the Chinese Canadian patients tended to utilize general practitioners and medical clinics rather than mental health clinics.

Hessler and associates (1975) conducted a survey of 200 households in Boston's Chinatown. The purpose of the study was to determine predictors of the kind of health care used by Chinese Americans. Predictor variables included (1) demographic variables (age, income, education, length of stay in the United States, citizenship status, marital status, employment status, and number of children), (2) medical beliefs (attitudes toward giving and receiving blood and the value of flu shots, chest X-rays, and yearly physical examinations), (3) ethnic solidarity (money sent to China, membership in family associations, personnel in local hospitals), and (4) previous medical experiences. Analysis was made of the discriminatory power of each of the four variables, taken singly and in combination, on type of health care used. Hessler and his colleagues distinguished four types of health care utilization patterns: (1) Chinese medicine only (that is, medical practitioners or healers who use Chinese medicine, such as herbs and proper food balance through the concept of Yin-Yang, or Chinese concepts involving body massage and manipulation), (2) predominantly Chinese medicine, (3) predominantly Western medicine, and (4) equal use of Western and Chinese medicine. The results of the study were highly complex. Interestingly, however, none of the respondents used Western medicine exclusively. The study showed that Chinese Americans have access to, and utilize, non-Western forms of health care that to some extent compete with Western medicine. The existence of non-Western health care has significance for our analysis of mental health. Lin and his associates (1978) found that Chinese Canadians tended to utilize medical treatment for psychological disturbances. As discussed later in this chapter, somatic and psychological distress in Asian cultures are often intertwined.

Gurin, Veroff, and Feld (1960), in their survey of mental health attitudes, found that most Americans seek help from clergymen and family physicians for emotional problems. We believe that Asian Americans rely on such culturally consistent forms of assistance as family, kinship, and herbalists, so that their utilization of mental health services is further reduced. This belief, however, has not been confirmed by research. We have not seen any studies that directly compare the willingness of Asian and Caucasian Americans to use mental health facilities.

Cost. Financial considerations are always important in decisions about service utilization. Owan (1975) had shown that among Japanese, Chinese, and Pilipino Americans, especially the males, in the cities of Los Angeles-Long Beach, San Francisco-Oakland, Seattle-Everett, Chicago, New York, and Boston, Chinese and Pilipinos had significantly lower median incomes than Whites. The issue is whether Asian Americans are less likely than Caucasian Americans to use services because of the cost of services. This does not seem to be a powerful explanation for underutilization by Asian Americans. Most mental health facilities consider one's ability to pay for services in determining fees. Moreover, Brown and associates (1973) reported a program whereby mental health services were offered free of charge at a community mental health center located in Chinatown, Los Angeles. There was no significant increase in admissions to the facility. Where financial considerations are likely to be prominent is in the distribution of monies according to service priorities. That is, individuals with severely limited incomes tend to use those services that are deemed necessary, while higher-income persons are freer to select more services. In a survey of Korean, Pilipino, Japanese, and Chinese Americans, Kim (1978) asked respondents to rate the importance of eight types of services: childcare centers, English conversation classes, mental health services, employment services, vocational training, public aid, bilingual referral services, and legal aid services. Mental health services received the lowest importance rating among the different services. One interpretation of Kim's finding is that Asian Americans have less need for mental health services since they are psychologically well adjusted. Another is that they have so many other important needs that mental health services are by necessity of lower relative priority. A third possibility is that mental health services are not well understood by Asian

Americans, since Western concepts involving mental health and psychotherapy are culturally inconsistent with their belief systems. The last two possibilities point to a potential discrepancy between mental health *needs* and mental health service *demands*. Needs may be high, but demands for services may be low.

Location and Knowledge of Facilities. Utilization of treatment services is generally influenced by location of the facility and knowledge of services. If facilities are not conveniently located, use of the facilities is discouraged. For Asian Americans who may have special needs for bilingual personnel, the problem is exacerbated. Since they are a relatively small minority group, few, if any, mental health facilities typically have personnel who can speak the various Asian languages. Consequently, those that do have bilingual staff must often serve clients who are located far away from the facilities. In the Seattle area, for example, Asian American clients may travel over 100 miles to use the Chinese Information and Service Center or the Asian Counseling and Referral Service. This kind of situation obviously discourages utilization.

Comprehensive community mental health centers operate under the catchment area concept. A center provides care to those persons who live in or near the community where the facility is located (Bloom, 1977). A catchment area generally encompasses 75,000 to 200,000 persons. A comprehensive community mental health center with bilingual staff may not be able to serve Asian American clients who live in a different catchment area. One solution to this problem would be to allow centers having special services that are not found in other centers to act as a magnet for clients needing the services, without regard to catchment area boundaries. It does not, however, address the issue of location, since clients may still have to travel great distances in order to find bilingual personnel. The need for bilingual personnel is especially critical when one considers that well over half of the Asian Americans are foreign born and that some Asian American groups (such as Vietnamese Americans) are composed almost exclusively of foreign-born individuals.

In view of the large numbers of foreign-born Asian Americans who have limited facility with English, many may simply not know where to receive mental health services or not know about the existence of such services. Kim (1978) found that a significant number of subjects—about 15 percent of the male and 20 percent of the female Chinese, Japanese, Pilipino, and Korean American respondents—did not seek help for problems primarily because they did not know where to go for the necessary services. Particularly affected were immigrants and women. However, adequate knowledge of services and access to facilities do not ensure utilization. They are necessary but not sufficient conditions for seeking and using professional mental health services.

Hours of Operation. Related to the issue of accessibility is the fact that many mental health facilities primarily operate (except for emergency services) during "normal" business hours. There is evidence that in Asian American families (compared to Caucasian Americans), a greater proportion of husbands and wives work, so that utilization may be discouraged by "normal" business hours (Sue, Sue, and Sue, 1975). Chinese Americans in Chinatown areas also tend to work extremely long hours, and it is not uncommon for those in restaurants or garment factories to have a ten- to fourteen-hour working day. However, although some potential clients may be affected by the limited hours of operation of services, the power of this explanation for differential use of facilities between Asian and Caucasian Americans is probably slight. Only a small proportion of Asian Americans live in Chinatowns, and many other Americans are also affected by hours of operation. Where hours of operation may be a factor is that, given the Asian American cultural attitude toward mental health care and the likelihood that the residents in the immigrant Asian American communities are employed by Asian Americans, it may be extremely difficult for those who wish to seek mental health care to get released from their jobs to do so.

Belief Systems About Mental Health. If one attributes feelings of distress to physical or somatic processes, he will seek medical forms of intervention. If the attribution is to psychological or interpersonal conflicts, psychotherapy or mental health care is more likely to be used. Thus, cultural beliefs and attributions are important to study, since they have implications for help-seeking behavior.

Sue and associates (1976) found that Asian Americans (Chinese, Japanese, and Pilipino Americans) were more likely than Caucasian Americans to believe that mental illness is caused by organic factors. Results also indicate that Asian Americans tend to believe that one achieves good mental health by avoiding morbid thoughts. Similarly, in an exploratory survey of Chinatown, San Francisco, Lum (1974) noted that Chinese Americans believe that mental health results from the exercise of will power and the avoidance of morbid thoughts. Arkoff, Thaver, and Elkind (1966) compared the responses of Asian foreign-born students with the responses of Caucasian American students. They found that the foreign-born students were more likely to believe in will power and pleasant thoughts as means of enhancing sound mental health.

These studies suggest that Asian and Caucasian Americans do have different conceptions of mental health and disturbance. Asian Americans tend to perceive more organic or somatic involvement in emotional disturbance. They also believe that the exercise of will power, the avoidance of morbid thoughts, and a focus on pleasant cognitions are means to enhance psychological well-being. Since professional mental health treatment often stresses insight-oriented approaches that require self-disclosure of "morbid" (that is, disturbing and embarrassing) thoughts, Asian Americans may avoid Western forms of mental health treatment and seek medical treatment for emotional problems.

Responsiveness of Services. If mental health services do not respond to the needs, values, or life-styles of clients, we would expect underutilization of services, premature termination of services among users, and poor therapeutic outcomes. We have found no studies of the efficacy of psychotherapeutic treatment with Asian versus Caucasian Americans; there is ample evidence, however, that Asian Americans underutilize services and drop out of treatment (President's Commission on Mental Health, 1978). As indicated earlier, Sue and McKinney

(1975) found that, out of 13,198 patients seen in seventeen community mental health centers in the greater Seattle area, only 100 were Asian Americans, a rate many times lower than their proportion in the surrounding population. Furthermore, 52 percent of the Asian American clients dropped out of treatment after one session, as compared to a 30 percent rate for White Americans. Asian Americans averaged 2.35 treatment sessions, a significant difference from the 7.96 average for White Americans.

These findings—coupled with what is known about stigma and shame, location and knowledge of services, and belief systems—indicate that the traditional service delivery system may be ill suited to serve Asian Americans. One of the major goals of the system is to reach the high-risk needy groups (Wu and Windle, 1980), so that aspirations for the system have clearly exceeded achievements.

As noted by the President's Commission on Mental Health (1978), the delivery system has failed to deal with cultural diversity among potential clients and to have sufficient numbers of bilingual personnel: "Too often, services which are available are not in accord with [the] cultural and linguistic traditions [of Asian and Pacific Island Americans]. The number . . . utilizing mental health services increases dramatically when services take into account their cultural traditions and patterns" (pp. 5-6). The basic issue is one of match or fit. To be of maximum benefit and value, there must be a match between the person and the service. Garfield (1974) advocates the consideration of therapist characteristics, client characteristics, situational variables, and the interaction of these factors in assessing the efficacy of treatment. In Chapter Five we discuss what we consider important combinations of factors for positive therapeutic outcomes. For the time being, our concern is that client characteristics (such as cultural diversity and linguistic facility) and therapist characteristics (for instance, knowledge of and experience with Asian American clients and bilingual ability) are often mismatched.

Wu and Windle (1980) conducted an interesting study on the use of community mental health centers by ethnic minority groups. They wanted to ascertain whether centers with minority group personnel tended to have more minority group clients than centers with few minority group staff. From data collected by the National Institute of Mental Health at 220 community mental health centers, the investigators selected centers that had over 2,000 individuals of a particular ethnic group (Native American, Asian American, Black, or Hispanic) in their catchment areas. For Asian Americans thirteen centers met this criterion. To calculate the relative utilization of the centers by Asian Americans, Wu and Windle divided the number of Asian American clients admitted to the center by the population of Asian Americans in the catchment areas. They made similar calculations to determine the relative utilization of the centers by Caucasian Americans. Finally, they calculated the relative staffing of Asian Americans in the centers by considering the number of hours reported for the Asian American staff at the centers in a sample week, the number of hours for White American staff, and the respective populations in the catchment areas. The relative utilization rate for Asian Americans was .23, which reveals a high degree of underutilization and which is not surprising in view of other studies demonstrating similar results. The relative staffing rate for Asian Americans was 1.01. Thus, they were not especially underrepresented in professional staff relative to White Americans. There was a direct relationship (although not significant) between the number of Asian American staff and the number of Asian American clients. On the basis of that finding, Wu and Windle suggest that minority group utilization of mental health services might be increased if minority group staff were increased.

Wu and Windle's finding that Asian Americans are not underrepresented in professional staff is at odds with the findings of the Asian American subpanel to the President's Commission on Mental Health (1978), which specifically noted the lack of bilingual and bicultural personnel. Wu and Windle's study, however, included only a small proportion of all federally funded community mental health centers—primarily those with large numbers of Asian Americans in the catchment areas. Moreover, Asian Americans are diverse, and the inclusion of a bilingual,

Korean-speaking staff member does not respond to the problems of, say, clients who speak Vietnamese. The issue of staffing, then, is complex. Some of the findings from Kim's (1978) survey are relevant. In her study Chinese, Japanese, Pilipino, and Korean Americans (immigrants and United States citizens) rated characteristics considered important in services. The existence of bilingual staff and the helpfulness of staff were the top-rated characteristics among a list that also included convenient access to services, confidentiality of services, and financial cost of services. Not surprisingly, immigrants considered bilingual staff more crucial than United States citizens did.

Untreated-Case Method of Determining
Rates of Disturbance

One major problem in the treated-case method is that treated persons are self-selected. The untreated-case method attempts to ascertain the extent of psychopathology by surveying all of a particular population or a sample of that population. Sampling, reliability of instruments, and validity are the major methodological problems when the untreated-case method is used to ascertain rates of psychopathology (Dohrenwend and Dohrenwend, 1974a). Sampling procedures must assure that the population characteristics are represented and that subject mortality or refusal to cooperate does not systematically bias the results. However, the most complex problem involves the validity of instruments to determine what constitutes mental disturbance. In comparisons across cultures or minority groups, attention must be paid to the validity of assessment tools, differential response sets, the stimulus value of assessment materials for respondents, and interpretations of the findings with respect to different cultures. The problem is that few mental health studies using untreated-case methods have been conducted. Four such studies will be discussed, each with different strengths and weaknesses. Two examine mental health issues as a function of personality test results, and two involve outcomes of needs assessment surveys.

Personality Tests. In the first study, Sue and Kirk (1973) compared Japanese and Chinese American college students with non-Asian students. In 1966 at the University of California, Berkeley, all entering freshmen were asked to participate in a testing program. Among the various tests administered, the Omnibus Personality Inventory (OPI) was taken by about 73 percent of the students. Sue and Kirk separated the American-born Chinese (N = 205) and Japanese (N = 95) from all other non-Asian students (control, N = 2,027). Race-by-sex comparisons were then made on the OPI. In terms of anxiety level, Chinese American males and females expressed significantly more discomfort than their control counterparts. On the Personal Integration Scale, Chinese American males and females and Japanese American males expressed more feelings of isolation and loneliness than their control counterparts. These three groups on the Social Extroversion Scale also had a greater tendency to withdraw from social contacts. Japanese American females did not differ from the control females on any of these scales. Finally, in their responses to the Impulse Expression Scale, Chinese American males and females and Japanese American females were more likely to inhibit the expression of impulses than control males and females. No differences between Chinese and Japanese Americans reached significance. These results suggest that Chinese American males and females and Japanese American males show feelings of anxiety, discomfort, loneliness, and isolation. They are less socially extroverted and less likely to express impulses than other students. The results are less clear for Japanese American females.

Taken at face value, the results imply that Asian American college students are more emotionally distressed than other college students. Since these students were not selected on the basis of help-seeking behavior, they represented a "normal" group of entering college students. They were also American-born Chinese and Japanese, so that the additional stress of immigration and adjustment was not present. Certainly, this study offers no support for the popular belief that Asian Americans are extremely well adjusted.

The second study (Cambra, Klopf, and Oka, 1978; see also Klopf and Cambra, 1979; Oka, Cambra, and Klopf, 1979) deals with the common observation among educators that Asian Americans tend to be verbally inhibited. Asian Americans often do not speak out in classes; and when they do speak, they often have difficulty in articulating in English. The problem does not seem to be caused by a lack of language facility or by a lack of novel ideas, interesting insights, or intelligent thoughts. Rather than having cognitive deficiencies, Asian Americans appear to be less verbal because of personality or situational variables: shyness, speech anxiety, conformity to authority figures, and reserve.

Cambra, Klopf, and Oka have argued that communication apprehension, defined as anxiety associated with talk (real or anticipated) with one or more persons, can have devastating consequences. Their review of the literature suggested that high communication apprehension is associated with lower college grade point averages, less social and sexual attractiveness, lowered self-esteem, reduced employment opportunities, less confidence and emotional maturity, social maladaptiveness, and general anxiety. In short, the investigators propose that high communication apprehension has negative impact on well-being.

Cambra and his colleagues studied the speech anxiety of University of Hawaii students, the vast majority of whom were Asian Americans. During the first week of classes, they administered the Personal Report of Communication Apprehension for College Students to those enrolled in speech courses. After students had completed the courses, they were readministered the Personal Report. Students did show a pre- to posttest reduction in speech anxiety. However, on the pretest measure, about 61 percent of the 703 students considered themselves above average in apprehension during oral communication situations; and 32 percent reported that they were almost always highly anxious. Students in Hawaii, compared with national norms, were found to exceed other college students in anxiety. For example, on the same self-report measure, only 20 percent of other student populations reported that they were almost always highly anxious. The investigators conclude that University of Hawaii students probably have the highest incidence of communication apprehension among the nation's universities. Since the vast majority of students in their study were Asian American and since Cambra and his associates link communication apprehension with a variety of indices of impaired mental health, a reasonable conclusion may be that Asian American students at the University of Hawaii have less than optimal mental health.

These studies are typical of many untreated-case methods used to compare the mental health of Asian and Caucasian Americans. They are instructive in that both studies challenge the notion that Asian Americans are exceedingly well adjusted, although neither research is particularly sophisticated in design. Since they dealt with special populations of college students— American-born Chinese and Japanese in the Sue and Kirk study and University of Hawaii speech students in the Cambra study— the generality of the findings is open to question. Though the appropriateness of the assessment instruments can also be questioned, the studies do include comparison groups, so that it is possible to view the performance of Asian Americans in perspective.

Regarding the appropriateness of assessment tools, Mizokawa and Morishima (1979) and Morishima and Mizokawa (1979) report that Japanese-speaking subjects may have difficulty with negative stems and colloquial expressions such as "neither here nor there." They point out that in Japanese *koko* means "here," *asoko* means "there," and *soko* refers to a point between the former and the latter. A Japanese-speaking subject, then, may have difficulty in interpreting that colloquial expression. Cordova (1974) found that one major difficulty faced by Pilipino immigrants in taking tests is the use of multiple-choice and mark-sense answer sheets. Pilipinos, unlike most Americans, have not had experience with multiple-choice formats, since examinations in Philippine institutions are typically in essay format. Pilipinos, then, need experience with multiple-choice formats and specific instructions on what is expected of the respondent when confronted with a mark-sense form.

A personality test may, therefore, create more anxiety, and the demands of the test may be perceived in a more ambiguous fashion for members of culture A than for those of culture B. If the two cultures perform differently on a test, it is unclear whether the difference should be attributed to real differences in personality attributes or to contaminating factors involving the test's stimulus value. Responses to questionnaires may also be determined by enduring personality dispositions that are different from and usually irrelevant to the kinds of traits the questionnaire has been designed to measure. Acquiescence and social desirability are common examples of response sets. Dohrenwend and Dohrenwend (1969), for instance, found that while Puerto Ricans scored higher than Jewish, Irish, or Black American respondents on a mental health symptom questionnaire, the Puerto Rican culture appeared to encourage greater expression of distress. Thus, a response set rather than actual underlying psychopathology may have accounted for the higher symptom score. In the absence of other evidence, it is difficult to interpret the findings of Sue and Kirk and of Cambra, Klopf, and Oka. Do they show that Asian Americans really are more emotionally disturbed than Caucasian Americans, or are the differences more apparent than real?

A final issue can be raised in the Cambra study. In pointing to a number of social, emotional, and economic factors associated with communication apprehension, the investgators suggest that University of Hawaii students (most of whom were Asian Americans) have problems that impair their mental health. The weakness in the interpretation is that speech anxiety may be highly situational and not reflective of serious underlying emotional problems. For example, in a study of Japanese American students at the University of Hawaii, Ayabe (1971) also noticed that these students participated in classroom discussions less than Caucasian American students did. He proposed two possible explanations: (1) Japanese Americans are physically unable to speak as loudly and forcefully as Caucasian Americans. (2) Japanese Americans show greater deference to authority figures. In either case, he believed, the speech of Japanese Americans would be inhibited. To test the two hypotheses, race of student (Japanese versus Caucasian), type of experimenter (professor versus another student), and request (speak as loudly as possible versus speak normally) were manipulated and voice was measured by a sound meter. In the "speak normally" condition, no racial differences were found; however, in the "speak loudly" condition, Japanese American students scored significantly lower in voice level than did Caucasian American students only in the presence of a professor. The findings suggest that Japanese American students may participate less in verbal discussions and perhaps have greater speech anxiety in the presence of authority figures. If this is the case, communication may be quite situation specific for Asian Americans. In contrast to Cambra's conclusions, speech anxiety may not signal pervasive socioemotional problems among Asian American students.

Dohrenwend and Dohrenwend (1969) also question the ability of surveys of communities to distinguish between situationally specific symptoms and psychological disorder. Symptoms may not always indicate the presence of a disorder.

Needs Surveys. Needs surveys are intended to provide data on the problems and needs of a specific group. They give insight into mental health but do not directly deal with rates of psychopathology. Among the best surveys of Asian American mental health needs are those reported by Kim (1978) and Prizzia and Villanueva-King (1977).

Kim studied Chinese, Japanese, Korean, and Pilipino Americans (immigrants and citizens) in the Chicago area. This study is a particularly good example of an Asian American needs assessment, even though the addition of a non-Asian American control group would have made the study even more useful.

The study gathered information on social, economic, educational, and mental health needs as well as attitudes and beliefs about social service organizations and cultural resources. Kim realized that she would have to address several problems in conducting the research. First, the target groups in Chicago were quite dispersed and relatively small in number, so that sampling and the selection of respondents would be extremely difficult. To find immigrants, she used the files from the Immigration and Naturalization Service and randomly selected immigrants from China, Japan, Korea, and the Philippines. Immigrants who were at least eighteen years of age, permanent residents, and living in

Chicago formed the population from which the sample was drawn. In the case of Chinese and Japanese Americans, Kim also wanted to sample United States citizens. In order to find subject pools, she used community informants, various ethnic directories, and census information indicating the geographical areas with Chinese and Japanese American concentrations. These sampling techniques may have introduced some systematic biases, but they were deemed necessary under the circumstances.

Kim decided to obtain information on respondents' (1) demographic background, (2) perception of problems and service needs, (3) perception of discrimination in employment and housing, (4) problem-solving strategies, (5) problems with health care, (6) reasons for immigration, and (7) sense of ethnic identity. Questionnaire items were translated into the different ethnic languages. They were also pretested for wording, structure, and meaning on a small group of respondents. The survey instrument was administered by interviewers of the same ethnic background as that of the respondents.

Some important findings emerged for the Asian American groups as a whole and for each group separately. English proficiency was of major concern, particularly to Chinese Americans. Lack of proficiency seemed to exacerbate virtually every problem area that Asian Americans perceived, and it also tended to limit the availability of problem-solving strategies. Adjustment to language and cultural differences was cited as a major problem; insufficient income, employment problems, and experiencing discrimination were also common problems. These difficulties were particularly expressed by immigrants, who, nevertheless, revealed few regrets over the decision to emigrate. The Japanese American citizens were the most likely to perceive racial discrimination, perhaps because World War II experiences in this country have sensitized them to discrimination.

The groups also showed differences in help-seeking behavior. In response to a hypothetical question regarding where they would seek help for mental "illness," Chinese Americans tended to select public resources (such as hospitals, doctors, or police) rather than private ones (such as family, friends, or relatives). Over one fourth of the respondents did not know where to go for help. On the other hand, Japanese Americans relied more heavily on private resources. Only 4 percent stated that they did not know where to go. Responses of the Pilipino and Korean Americans tended to fall between those of the Chinese and Japanese Americans. While mental health services were considered low priority, legal aid was rated first among services. Although there is no evidence that Asian Americans have a high need for legal aid, Kim believes that legal matters may be of particular concern to those who find the legal system (contracts, legal rights, law enforcement) strange and frightening.

The study does not, and was not intended to, address the frequency of mental disturbance. It is, nevertheless, a pioneering effort in trying to overcome realistic problems in Asian American research and in providing insight into the needs, attitudes, and behaviors of four Asian American groups. The prominence of English-language and cultural adjustment problems for these groups (especially immigrants) implies that they are under stress; these problems have major implications for mental health, career opportunities, day-to-day living, the general quality of life, and help-seeking behaviors.

The second needs survey (Prizzia and Villanueva-King, 1977) was conducted in Hawaii. In many ways Hawaii is an ideal location to conduct research on Asian Americans. Over 60 percent of the population is composed of Asian and Pacific Island Americans; there is a substantial representation of different ethnic groups; the population includes recent immigrants as well as generations of Hawaii-born Asian Americans; location of subjects for follow-up studies is facilitated by the limited mobility of subjects on the islands. Not surprisingly, therefore, Hawaii has been the site for many cross-cultural research studies.

Some of these advantageous factors, however, also limit the generality of findings. For example, Ogawa (1973) argues that Japanese Americans in Hawaii differ from their mainland counterparts. Their identity is formed not only by their Japanese and American backgrounds but also by the interrelationships of cultures in Hawaii. So strong is the influence of local cultures that many Japanese Americans identify primarily with living in Hawaii and only secondarily with being Japanese or

American. Because of the relatively large proportions of Asian Americans from diverse Asian groups in an island state where no majority group (in numbers) exists, there is less likely to be an "Asian American" identity. Furthermore, the White-majority versus Asian American–minority phenomenon present on the mainland is absent in Hawaii, and the social and psychological implications of this fact are undoubtedly substantial. To some extent, studies on Hawaii must be carefully scrutinized because of these factors.

Prizzia and Villanueva-King (1977) were interested in gaining information on mental health problems and service needs of residents in central Oahu (which includes Honolulu). Face-to-face interviews were conducted with over 900 respondents randomly selected from designated areas. Demographic information, reports on the respondent's life (experiences related to mental health), and opinions regarding mental health were obtained.

Results indicated some major ethnic differences:

1. *Awareness of Services.* Relative to other social and health services, mental health facilities were not as well known. About 40 percent of the respondents were familiar with the community counseling center. No major ethnic differences in awareness were apparent.

2. *Importance of Counseling Services.* A very high percentage (95 percent of the respondents) felt that counseling services were important or very important. Among specific kinds of services, treatment, especially for chronic and serious problems, was considered more important than self-improvement or self-help services. Interestingly, Samoan, Pilipino, and Hawaiian Americans considered counseling more important than did Chinese, Japanese, and Caucasian Americans. The researchers speculate that those latter groups are more affluent and probably consider state-sponsored counseling services less important.

3. *Comfort in Using Services.* When asked about how they would feel about going to a Department of Health counseling center, about one third of the respondents indicated

they would feel some degree of discomfort. Ranked in descending order were Samoan, Pilipino, Hawaiian, Chinese, Caucasian, and Japanese Americans.

4. *Preferences in Personnel.* Hawaiian, Pilipino, and Samoan Americans tended to be more comfortable with nurses and counselors than with psychologists and psychiatrists. The opposite was true for Caucasian, Japanese, and Chinese Americans. Perhaps because of their higher socioeconomic status in Hawaii, the latter groups may simply have more access to psychologists and psychiatrists. An alternative explanation is that, because of certain cultural values, the former groups feel less comfortable with psychologists and psychiatrists.

5. *Types of Problems.* When respondents were asked to indicate causes of stress, the following problems were rated in descending order of stress: money problems, job pressures, children's behavior, intrafamily communications, school problems, unemployment, in-law problems, crowding, drinking (alcohol), cultural differences in the family, and the desire to return to home country or state. Ethnicity was not very important in accounting for variation on this scale.

6. *Contact.* The adequacy of contacts with family and friends was assessed. Only 1 percent felt that there was not enough contact, and ethnicity was not an important factor in response.

7. *Life Satisfaction.* Only 3 percent of the respondents indicated that they were dissatisfied with their lives. Asian and Caucasian American groups showed little differences in responses.

8. *Help Seeking.* When asked how they handle stress, subjects indicated the following sources of help, in descending order of frequency of help sought: immediate family, priest, professional help from public sources, and psychiatrists. There appears to be an inverse relationship between the help-seeking behaviors of respondents and the degree of mental health training of the source. Propensity to use coping mechanisms was assessed. Pilipino and Chinese Americans

exhibited a lower propensity to use the coping strategies assessed by the survey.

This needs assessment is interesting for several reasons. In many areas ethnic differences did not seem very important. Awareness of services, types of problems, contact, and life satisfaction did not yield strong ethnic differences. When ethnic differences did occur, Samoan, Hawaiian, and Pilipino Americans usually differed from Chinese, Japanese, and Caucasian Americans, who generally had higher levels of income and education. In their help-seeking behavior, respondents are least likely to use professional mental health workers, with family and friends the preferred choice as helping agents.

Critical Discussion

At the beginning of this chapter, two opposing views of the mental health of Asian Americans were presented. In one perspective, advocated by some social scientists, Asian Americans are extremely well adjusted and mentally healthy. The opposing view is that Asian Americans experience significant mental health problems, which for one reason or another have gone unnoticed. Until recently we felt that careful and systematic research would resolve the controversy. We now believe that the issue cannot be meaningfully resolved by the methodologies and strategies used in the studies cited. That is, previous investigations have actually shed little light on the rates of psychopathology for Asian Americans; in the absence of definitive research, however, these studies have acted as projective stimuli whereby investigators are free to draw whatever conclusions they deem appropriate. Hence, there is a continuing controversy. In our view, the use of treated cases as a means for estimating mental health is so seriously flawed that it should be discontinued. The untreated-case method is not dependent on help-seeking behavior, so that it has a great deal of potential. Its potential, however, has not yet been fully realized, especially in making cross-cultural comparisons.

We believe that the question of the rates of mental disturbance is interesting, has scientific value, and has obvious policy implications. Nevertheless, in the absence of more definitive research, further efforts should not be expended in arguing what the rates are. More time should be spent on the development of alternative strategies. We suggest three areas of investigation that may be fruitful. First, the untreated-case method should be developed so that more meaningful findings can be achieved. Second, since rates of mental disturbance are influenced by stressors and resources, these two classes of factors must be better understood. A major part of this book is devoted to Asian American stressors and resources. Third, insight into mental health can be facilitated by knowledge of cultural differences in symptomotology or in the expression of disorders. This issue is discussed in the next chapter.

3

Recognizing Symptoms and Identifying Disturbed Persons

By studying cross-cultural variations in the expression of mental disturbance, one can often gain an understanding of the relationship between disturbance, socialization practices, and treatment effectiveness. That cultural experiences influence symptoms is not surprising. Important issues concern (1) the nature of symptom expression for different cultures, (2) the means by which symptom expression and disorder are conceptualized, and (3) implications for Asian Americans.

Kleinman (1977) contrasts two models for studying psychiatric disorders in different societies: the transcultural model and the new cross-cultural perspective. Transcultural psychiatry attempts to find universals or common elements of particular disorders across different cultures. Without these universals, it is difficult to make cross-cultural comparisons and to determine whether the same disorder is being investigated in different cultures. For example, unless schizophrenia shows common symptoms or underlying processes in Cultures A and B, the disorder has little meaning for cross-cultural purposes. In an attempt to resolve the problem, transcultural psychiatry tends to impose criteria or categories; behaviors in different cultures that meet the criteria or fit into the categories are then deemed to be indicators of equivalent disorders.

At first glance, the transcultural approach seems reasonable. Kleinman's objection is that culture-specific factors may determine the criteria or categories of behaviors. Calling the problem a *category fallacy*, he notes its effects in the case of depression: "Applying such a category to analyze cross-cultural studies, or even in direct field research, is *not* a cross-cultural study of depression, because by definition it will *find* what is 'universal' and systematically *miss* what does not fit its tight parameters. The former is what is defined and therefore 'seen' by a Western cultural model; the latter, which is not so defined and therefore not 'seen,' raises far more interesting questions for cross-cultural research. It is precisely in the latter group that one would expect to find the most striking examples of the influence of culture on depression" (p. 4).

Kleinman's position is that the very act of defining criteria and categories to assess behaviors in different cultures may obscure the influence of culture. The challenge is not so much to develop criteria for disorders on the basis of symptoms; the central task is to discover the underlying disorder while appreciating cultural influences on the expression of symptoms. How can this be accomplished?

Kleinman's ideal cross-cultural study would entail detailed and local phenomenological descriptions. Comparisons between indigenous and professional psychiatric or psychological explanations of disorders could be made. Independent of a unified interpretive framework, symptom terms and illness labels would be compared. The major task is to translate these local accounts so that a comparative model for cross-cultural comparisons can emerge.

Kleinman (1979) has proposed a model of illness as shown in Figure 1. While the model is used primarily to apply to his work on depression, it is relevant to psychopathology in general.

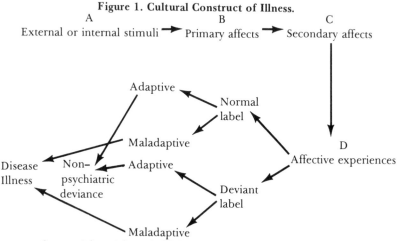

Figure 1. Cultural Construct of Illness.

Source: Adapted from A. Kleinman. Copyright 1979 by University of California Press, Berkeley.

In Kleinman's model, affects (emotions) are fundamental psychological phenomena engendered in an individual by external (for example, interpersonal) stimuli and internal (for example, intrapsychic or somatic) stimuli. Those stimuli giving rise to intense or dysphoric affects are stressors (environmental, social, psychological, or physiological). Even at this level of Kleinman's model, cultural influences are important, since they partly determine which stimuli are stressors and how potent the stressors are. The stressors lead to primary affects: essential psychobiological phenomena that have physiological correlates and are universal (across cultures). Primary affective states are "uncognized," occurring prior to cognition. Once labeled or interpreted (for instance, as anger or sadness), the primary affects become secondary affects. Social and cultural factors play a vital role in cognition, the interpretation of primary affects, and the particular expression of secondary (cognized) affects. While primary affective states are universal, secondary ones are culture specific. Secondary affects result in affective experiences that are either socially sanctioned as "normal" or labeled as "deviant." Either category (normal or deviant) may include personal adaptive or maladaptive processes. Maladaptive normal or deviant affective experiences may be further classified as disease/illness, while adaptive deviant experiences fall into a class of nonpsychiatric deviance.

Cultural influences are important at all levels of this model, except at the primary affective stage. They determine the impact of stressors that influence primary affects, the self-labeling and experience of primary affects in the form of secondary affects, the nature of affective experiences that are considered by others as normal or deviant, the experiences that are personally adaptive or maladaptive, and, finally, the experiences that are classified as disease/illness or nonpsychiatric deviance.

Kleinman's model is intriguing in its attempt to fully appreciate the pervasiveness of culture on psychopathology and to serve as an approach for cross-cultural research. It points to the cultural relativity of specific etiology, course, onset, symptoms, and treatment. Kleinman suggests that indigenous and professional psychiatric descriptions and explanations be used to develop conceptual models so that decisions on disorders and their comparability can be subsequently made. In this way, inferences may be drawn as to the occurrence of primary affects.

By pointing to the importance of local phenomenological descriptions of disorders in each culture, Kleinman adopts a relativistic perspective that emphasizes the need to understand disorders within each cultural context. Thus, he believes that traditional Western nosological systems may be inappropriate or biased for non-Western societies.

Kleinman's model is, however, difficult to operationalize because of the difficulty in deciding what the underlying disorder is for culturally determined symptoms. In medicine a diagnosis is rendered on the basis of the etiology, onset, course of the disorder, symptom-syndrome patterns, or response to specific treatment. For example, if a person is known to have neurosyphilis (etiology) and shows certain classic signs (symptoms) of the disorder, then we can be reasonably sure that the person is suffering from the disorder regardless of cultural background. Similarly, if a patient has one of two different diseases, and if each disease responds to a different specific treatment, one can determine which disease the patient has. Unfortunately, most mental disorders do not have specific treatments, and the physiological or organic substratum for most disorders is un-known.

In their review of cross-cultural research on psychopathology, Dohrenwend and Dohrenwend (1974a) raise four questions: (1) Do the kinds of disorders found in Western societies exist in non-Western cultures, or are Western classifications simply inapplicable? (2) If the Western classifications of the types of psychopathology do apply, are the distributions of these types the same or different in all cultures? (3) Are there new kinds or types of psychopathology found in non-Western cultures? (4) Are there different symptom manifestations of types of psychopathology found in all cultures? In contrast to Kleinman, the Dohrenwends conclude that Western diagnostic categories can be appropriately applied to non-Western cultures. Moreover, they believe that different cultural groups probably do have different distributions with respect to types of psychopathology, that different cultural groups may manifest different symptoms of a disorder, and that the issue of whether new types of disorders exist in non-Western cultures (but not in Western cultures) cannot be resolved at this time. Dohrenwend and Dohrenwend essentially adopt a relative rather than an absolute position with respect to symptom expression and to the distribution of types of mental disorder. However, they maintain that Western nosological systems can be applied across cultures.

We agree with the conclusions of the Dohrenwends. However, Western classification systems (and all other universally applied classification systems) are biased. Culture-free classification systems do not exist. By noting the limitations of these systems, by taking into consideration cultural relativity, and by constantly adapting classifications for greater scientific and clinically applied utility, one can classify psychopathology across cultures. Kleinman's ideas are valuable because they accentuate the need to consider cultural factors.

The questions raised by Dohrenwend and Dohrenwend are important to examine in the case of Asian Americans, particularly the ones concerning symptom manifestations (whether persons who are from different cultures have different symptoms for the same disorder) and the distribution of disorders (whether different cultural groups exhibit different incidence rates for specific forms of psychopathology; for example, is the incidence of schizophrenia the same in Cultures A and B?). While relevant empirical studies on these two questions are sparse, we want to indicate the available research findings.

Symptom Expression Among Asian Americans

The influence of culture in symptomatic behavior was well illustrated by Opler (1967), who found that hospitalized male schizophrenic patients from Italian and Irish American backgrounds differed in symptoms even though they suffered from the same disorder. For example, the Italian American group of patients exhibited more overt homosexuality and fewer fixed delusions than the Irish American group. Differences in symptomotology also have been noted among various Asian American groups. For example, Finney (1963) found that various ethnic groups in Hawaii tend to use different kinds of defense mechanisms. Enright and Jaeckle (1963) analyzed the behavioral patterns of Japanese and Pilipino American patients diagnosed as paranoid schizophrenics in the Hawaii State Hospital. Results indicated that the Japanese American group expressed more depression, withdrawal, disturbance in thinking, and inhibition, while the Pilipino Americans exhibited greater delusions of persecution and overt signs of disturbed behavior. These studies support the notion that disorders may be manifested differently, according to cultural or ethnic background.

Are certain specific modes of expressing distress more common among Asian Americans than Caucasian Americans? Clinical practitioners often remark that Asian or Asian American clients are more likely than Caucasian Americans to exhibit somatic symptoms, such as headaches, weakness, pressures on the chest or head, insomnia, and tenseness. Several lines of evidence suggest that somatic complaints frequently accompany psychological disturbance among Asians and Asian Americans. In an analysis of the kinds of psychopathology shown by Pilipino nationals serving in the U.S. Navy, Duff and Arthur (1967) conclude that many Pilipinos with mental disorders present somatic problems as well as feelings of shame and guilt. To determine whether ethnicity accounts for different symptom patterns in depression, Marsella, Kinzie, and Gordon (1973) administered a self-report checklist to Chinese, Japanese, and Caucasian American students who had scored high on the Zung Self-Rating Depression Scale. They found that Chinese Americans were the most likely to exhibit somatic symptoms in depression. In studying the Chinese in Taiwan, Kleinman (1977) and Kleinman and Sung (1979) have argued that Chinese throughout the world, particularly those suffering from depression, tend to present somatic complaints in place of psychological complaints.

The tendency for Chinese and Japanese American students to report somatic symptoms was investigated by Sue and Sue (1974), who compared the responses of Chinese and Japanese American college students with those of Caucasian American students on the MMPI items indicating somatic complaints. The students were drawn from the population of students utilizing a university psychiatric clinic. Even when these two groups were equated on severity of disturbance, the Asian Americans had a significantly higher mean endorsement of somatic complaint items than did Caucasian Americans. Rahe and associates (1978) found that, on the Cornell Medical Index, Vietnamese refugees in the United States tended to express psychological strain through somatic complaints. Finally, Sue and colleagues (1976) hypothesized that Asian Americans may have different perspectives of deviance than Caucasian Americans. In comparing the mental health attitudes of Asian and Caucasian Americans, these investigators found that Asian Americans were more likely to believe that mental disturbance is associated with organic or somatic factors; that is, Asian Americans may view mental and physical health as more interrelated than Caucasian Americans do.

How can the relationship between somatic complaints and mental disturbance be interpreted? There are at least three ways of interpreting the high frequency of somatic complaints. One possibility is that the complaints represent a cultural means of verbally expressing psychological distress. That is, Asian

Americans do not have more somatic problems than Caucasian Americans do; they simply complain more, or they are more likely to use physical referents for psychological distress. In our society one often speaks of a "broken heart," referring to an unsuccessful romance rather than to the physical status of one's heart. The interpretation that Asian Americans complain more, however, is not well supported. When Asian Americans complain about somatic symptoms, there is every indication that those physical problems are genuinely experienced as physical sickness. Many of the complaints are detailed, and Asian Americans often feel that if the physical problems were eliminated, there would be no further difficulty.

Whereas the first explanation has to do primarily with increased self-reporting behaviors, the other two explanations lie on a continuum with respect to the "realness" of the physical complaints. On one end of the continuum is the perspective that somatic complaints are solely a reflection of emotional disturbance—that physical problems are in one's "head" (imaginary) and not in one's body. Such a perspective denies the legitimacy of somatic concerns and implies (1) that removing the underlying cause (emotional disturbance) will eliminate the physical complaints and (2) that treating the physical complaints will accomplish very little, since the underlying cause is unaffected (and, indeed, symptom substitution may occur). At the other end of the continuum, the alternative perspective is that physical or somatic complaints are valid. One cannot easily separate physical from psychological functions. In this view, treatment should be aimed at the body and the mind. As pointed out by Kleinman and Sung (1979) in their study of the effectiveness of shaman in treating patients, successful treatment of mental disorders often requires intervention at the levels of disease (primary malfunctioning in biological and psychological processes) and of illness (secondary psychosocial and cultural responses to disease). To see physical complaints solely as a reflection of an underlying emotional problem is to deny the legitimacy of cultural patterns of expressing emotional disorders. We believe that the depressive syndrome (lack of energy, sadness, insomnia, motor retardation) exhibited in American or

Western culture is not a more valid, intrinsic, or sophisticated means of expressing depression than the somatization shown in other cultures. Why do Asian American groups tend to express emotional disorders by somaticization? We offer the following speculations. First, some Asian American groups may tend to see a unity between physical and psychological status; consequently, factors such as diet, exercise, leading a "good" life, achievement, and discipline are perceived to have consequences for the mind and the body (Wu, 1980). That is, if one's culture emphasizes a holistic view of psychological and physical health, both emotional and somatic problems are likely to be generated by stressors. Second, Kleinman (1977) believes that certain Asian groups tend to control self-disclosure or expression of strong affects such as dysphoria. Physical complaints may then be used to allow expression of personal and interpersonal problems. Third, for most Asian and Asian American groups, mental disturbance is highly stigmatized (Murase, 1980; Shon, 1980a). Mental disturbance reflects poorly on one's family and one's heredity and can lead to beliefs that the family's offspring are unfit for marriage. Under such circumstances, physical complaints have less negative consequences than emotional complaints, which imply mental disturbance.

In conclusion, cultural background does influence the expression of symptoms. There is evidence that Asian Americans, particularly Chinese Americans, exhibit somatic complaints in relation to psychological disturbance. Although some mental health professionals have proposed that Asian Americans also exhibit more guilt and shame, more paranoid patterns, and lower acting-out patterns (some of which will be discussed later in this book) than Caucasian Americans, there appear to be no definitive studies on these other attributes.

Distribution of Disorders Among Asian Americans

Do Asian Americans have the same proportion of specific disorders (such as depression, schizophrenia, or personality disorders) as Caucasian Americans? This issue is difficult to address. Since Asian Americans underutilize mental health services, the sample sizes of diagnosed Asian Americans are smaller and more self-selected than is usually the case. The sample sizes are significantly reduced further when specific Asian American groups are singled out. If Asian American groups are combined, then differences among these groups cannot be observed, and the within-group variance may be increased. Furthermore, it is unclear how valid the widely used classification systems for mental disorders (see the *Diagnostic and Statistical Manual* of the American Psychiatric Association, 1968 and 1980 editions) are in making comparisons between different groups. According to Sue (1977a), Asian American clients do not seem to exhibit large differences from Caucasian American clients in diagnoses. However, among users of mental health services, Asian Americans are more likely to receive psychotic diagnoses than Caucasian Americans are. This difference may be attributable to the fact that the less severely disturbed Asian Americans avoid using mental health services. As a result, the relatively smaller number who do use mental health services may be more highly disturbed. In other words, the question concerning possible differences in the distribution of disorders cannot be answered because few studies address the question, and the methodological problems (such as those resulting from small and more self-selective samples) have not been adequately resolved. Table 4 shows the distributions of disorders for various groups in the study by Sue (1977a).

High-Risk Asian American Populations

The Elderly. Interesting facts about Asian American elderly were revealed in a technical report by the Special Services for Groups (1978). First, Chinese and Japanese American elderly in California and Hawaii appear to have longer life expectancies than do Caucasian Americans. Second, while the total elderly population in the United States is increasing, the Chinese, Japanese, and Pilipino American elderly populations are growing even faster, probably because of the large numbers of elderly immigrants. Third, most elderly Asian Americans are foreign born. Fourth, the male:female ratio among Asian American

Table 4. Percentages of Diagnosis at Intake.

Diagnosis	Blacks**	Native Americans	Asian-Americans	Chicanos	Whites
Mental retardation	1.8	2.7	1.7	1.8	2.3
Organic brain syndrome	2.4	1.4	1.7	1.8	1.5
Psychosis	13.8	17.6	22.4	14.5	12.7
Neurosis	11.6	12.2	19.0	16.4	12.8
Personality disorder	33.3*	18.9	15.5	25.5	14.2
Psychophysiological	0	0	0	0	.3
Transient situational	15.0*	17.6	13.8	14.5	22.5
Behavior disorder	3.0	4.1	0	0	3.9
Other	19.1*	25.5	25.9	25.5	29.8
n	507	74	58	55	794

Note: Comparisons were made by using chi-squares.
*$p < .01$.
**$p < .001$.
Source: Sue (1977a); Copyright 1977 by the American Psychological Association. Reprinted by permission.

elderly is much higher than that among elderly populations in the United States. Fifth, compared to the total elderly population, a greater percentage of Asian American males are single or married with wives absent. Sixth, Asian American elderly have lower-status jobs, lower median incomes, and proportionally fewer persons receiving Social Security benefits than the total elderly population. These findings point to the fact that Asian American elderly face not only the problems associated with aging but also additional difficulties because of their unique characteristics as an elderly population. Fujii (1980) believes that elderly Asian Americans have received very little attention and that more appropriate knowledge and social services must be developed.

Peralta and Horikawa (1978) studied the elderly in the greater Philadelphia area. After interviewing over 250 elderly Chinese, Japanese, Korean, and Pilipino Americans, they concluded that elderly Asian Americans are economically disadvantaged and underutilize available public financial assistance and social services. Specifically, the elderly lack adequate English-speaking ability, find it difficult to negotiate the bureaucratic system, and avoid social services because the services often are not responsive to Asian American needs. The Asian American elderly, therefore, constitute a population with high mental health needs and with few resources (Chu, personal communication, 1981).

Wives of United States Servicemen. Since the end of World War II, nearly 200,000 Asian women have come to the United States as "war brides" of United States servicemen (Kim, 1977). Entering primarily from Japan, Korea, the Philippines, and Vietnam, these women encounter many problems and conflicts. Their families and communities are frequently quite negative over their associating with United States servicemen. The United States military and consulates also tend to discourage marriage applications. The most serious problems between husbands and wives, however, occur in the United States. The wives must often deal with isolation from familiar family and friends, homesickness, difficulty in obtaining ethnic food, lack of English proficiency, negative reactions toward interracial marriage, and a foreign culture. Many of these women experience marital strain, depression, fear, and even physical abuse from their husbands.

Eurasians. Interracial marriages between Asians/Asian Americans and Caucasian Americans are increasing. Many offspring of such marriages ("Eurasians") are now young adults who encounter special problems. Unlike the children of Black-White or Black/Asian/Asian American marriages, who are usually defined by others and by themselves as being Black, Eurasians may be perceived as alien and threatening to both Asian and Caucasian American cultural groups. In an interview of twenty-nine Eurasians between the ages of seventeen and twenty-one, Moritsugu, Foerster, and Morishima (1978) found that many Eurasians may be experiencing alienation because of their mixed ancestry. In other personality aspects, however, self-descriptions were quite positive (such as sensitive, curious, dependable, and honest). It is obvious that much more research is

necessary to determine the precise kinds of difficulties perceived by Eurasians. In fact, the need to research Eurasians is
great, and few investigators have attempted to do so.

Indochinese. Since 1975 nearly 300,000 Indochinese
refugees—primarily from Vietnam, Laos, and Cambodia—have
been admitted to the United States. That these refugees have
potential mental health problems is difficult to dispute. Prior to
coming to the United States, many of them were victims of war,
famine, revolutions, invasions, and internal political turmoil in
their native lands (Indochinese Consultation Committee, 1980).
Survival was a problem; families and communities were disrupted. Even the transit to the United States was ill planned.
Family members were frequently separated, and 85 percent of
the 130,000 refugees who came here in 1975 had between two
hours to two days to prepare to leave (Long, 1980).

Many of the refugees stayed in preliminary camps before
arriving in the United States. Camp Pendleton served as one of
the major refugee camps in the United States. Rahe and associates (1978) and Liu and Murata (1978) studied the mental
health of the refugees in Camp Pendleton. Problems of depression, anxiety, frustration, and suicide increased over time. In a
study of the Vietnamese in Denver, Aylesworth, Ossorio, and
Osaki (1980) have also concluded that the Vietnamese experience a great deal of depression and somatic problems. Even
though they have mental health problems, however, Wong
(1980) found that the Indochinese tend not to use mental
health services, a tendency found among most Asian American
groups.

Pacific Americans. Munoz (1980) and Luce (1980) have
recently articulated the plight of Pacific Americans, such as
those from Hawaii, Samoa, Fiji, Guam, and the United States
Trust Territories. These Pacific Islanders are undergoing rapid
social change through intermarriage, migration, and exposure to
other cultures and values. Many Pacific Americans in the United
States encounter problems with English, the educational system, employment, and culture conflict (Shu and Satele, 1977).
In a study by Yamamoto and Satele (1979), Samoan Americans
reported greater symptoms of disturbance than a non-Samoan

American control group. In many ways the concerns of Pacific Americans have received less attention than those of other Asian American groups.

Special Mental Health Problems

Let us briefly turn to research on specific mental health problems, such as alcoholism, drug abuse, suicide, and juvenile delinquency, since there is growing interest in how these problems affect Asian Americans. Good empirical data in these areas are not available; the findings, particularly for suicide, are inconsistent; and information concerning Asian American groups has focused primarily on Chinese and Japanese Americans, the two Asian American groups with the longest histories in the United States (with the exception, of course, of the Hawaiian Americans). The purpose in our presentation here is not to give an in-depth or comprehensive summary. Rather, our discussion is designed to highlight the major gaps in the empirical literature and to illustrate the diverse mental health needs and problems that face Asian Americans.

Alcohol Consumption. A number of investigators have suggested that certain Asian American groups have low rates of alcohol consumption and alcoholism. To account for the low rates, two explanations have been proposed: (1) genetic-racial differences in alcohol sensitivity and aversion and (2) ethnic-cultural differences in attitudes and values toward the use of alcohol. Studies by Wolff (1972) and by Ewing, Rouse, and Pellizzari (1974) have supported the genetic hypothesis. Wolff tested the reactivity to alcohol consumption between adult Caucasians (United States) and Asians (Japan, Taiwan, and Korea). In an attempt to control cultural differences in diet and other postnatal environmental influences, he also tested Caucasian, Japanese, and Chinese infants. Asian adults and infants were far more likely to exhibit face flushing than Caucasians were after the ingestion of alcohol. Moreover, reports of dysphoria and dizziness were more frequent among Asian than Caucasian adults, even when Caucasian subjects drank more alcohol per body weight. The Ewing study utilized Caucasian, Chinese,

Japanese, Korean, and South Vietnamese students, all residing in the United States. In response to alcohol consumption, Asians exhibited significantly greater face flushing and heart rate than Caucasians did.

In contrast to the genetic interpretation, several investigators (Barnett, 1955; Chu, 1972; DeVos, 1978) believe that certain Asian cultural values emphasize moderate drinking; excessive drinking is discouraged and tightly regulated by the family and community. As indicated by Sue, Zane, and Ito (1979, p. 44), differentiating between the genetic and cultural models is extremely difficult for several reasons: "First, hereditary differences may exist between races. Cultural values may be adopted in response to these differences. That is, cultural and even moral values against excessive drinking may have evolved because of one group's adverse physiological reaction. Second, genetic racial differences, such as flushing, may exist but may not influence drinking patterns. Third, cultural proscriptions against excessive alcohol consumption may form the basis for observed or self-reported physiological reactions. Self-reports of dizziness, nausea, and the like, may be culturally learned responses to alcohol. Finally, both genetic and cultural factors may influence drinking patterns. In any event, these two factors are almost inextricably confounded.

Sue, Zane, and Ito hypothesized that if culture is an important variable in alcohol consumption, then more assimilated Asian Americans should report greater alcohol consumption than less assimilated ones. By administering a questionnaire to Asian and Caucasian American subjects, the researchers found that (1) Asian Americans reported less alcohol consumption than Caucasians did, even after controlling for body weight differences between the two groups; (2) they also reported more face flushing in response to alcohol consumption than did Caucasians; and (3) assimilation measures for Asian Americans were directly related to the amount of reported consumption. The results, therefore, supported the cultural hypothesis, although the research did not shed light on the genetic interpretation. Taken at face value, the findings suggest that alcohol consumption (and perhaps alcoholism) may be lower among Asian Americans but that the rate may increase as a function of socialization processes (Kitano, 1981).

Drug Abuse. Little is known about the nature and extent of substance (nonalcohol) abuse among the various Asian American groups. At the First National Asian American Conference on Drug Abuse Prevention (Multicultural Drug Abuse Prevention Resource Center, 1976), participants generally felt that drug abuse is as prevalent in Asian American communities as in other communities. Nakagawa and Watanabe (1973) conducted a survey of over 700 Asian American students in Seattle junior and senior high schools. The purpose of the survey was to ascertain the extent of drug use (excluding marijuana and alcohol) among those students. Interestingly, more females (17 percent) than males (12 percent) were classified from the survey as drug users. By ethnicity, 49 percent of the "other" Asian Americans, 45 percent of the Pilipino Americans, 29 percent of the Japanese Americans, and 22 percent of the Chinese Americans had had some experience with drugs, including amphetamines, barbiturates, psychedelics, cocaine, and heroin (in descending order of frequency of use). The authors concluded that drug problems do exist among the youths in the Seattle Asian American community.

In the past, Chinese Americans in the United States have been burdened with stereotypes that associate them with the use of heroin and opium, tong wars, gambling, and prostitution. While these activities did form a part of the history of the Chinese Americans in the United States, the actual extent of and the reasons for drug usage have never been examined in detail. Lyman (1977) believes that organized drug dealings in Chinatowns provided revenues for the tongs and gained a foothold because many of the early Chinese immigrants were lonely and uncared for. To some extent, Ball and Lau (1966) also agree that many Chinese narcotic addicts were persons who were not well integrated into American society. They attribute this lack of integration to societal discrimination and restrictions on alternate modes of behavior. By examining 137 records of the 800 narcotic addicts at the U.S. Public Health Hospital in Kentucky from 1957 to 1962, Ball and Lau came up with a typical profile of the Chinese addict: mean age 53; immigrant from China; limited facility with English; and lack of recreational, spiritual, and social outlets. According to Ball and Lau, as well as Lyman, this pattern of heroin addiction is largely a phenomenon of the past.

Suicide. Statistics on suicide are subject to a number of biases and errors. It is often difficult to ascertain whether a particular death should be classed as a suicide. In the case of Asian Americans, little is known about suicide rates. Even the conclusions about one Asian American group, the Chinese Americans, are apparently inconsistent. Sung (1967) has indicated that Chinese Americans generally turn family discord and unhappiness inward toward the self, as reflected in high suicide rates. She states that the rate for Chinese Americans in San Francisco is four times greater than the rate for the city as a whole and that Chinese American women rather than men tend to commit suicide. Tom (1968) notes that while the suicide rate in San Francisco has been among the highest in the nation, Chinatown has even a higher rate than the rest of the city.

Two other social scientists have concluded that the suicide rate for Chinese Americans is lower than that of other groups. On the Hawaiian island of Oahu, Hsu (1970) found that the annual rate of suicide and attempted suicide of Chinese Americans was only one third of the rate for Caucasian Americans between 1957 and 1968. He concludes (in contrast to Sung) that Chinese Americans share life's ups and downs with families and friends, so that misery is not so unbearable. Analyzing data from the San Francisco coroner's office for 1952 to 1968, Bourne (1973) drew several conclusions with respect to the incidence of suicide among Chinese Americans: (1) Over the sixteen-year period, the mean rate of suicide for San Francisco Chinese Americans approximated that of the city at large. (2) The Chinese American rate, which two decades earlier was significantly higher than that of the non–Chinese American, had gradually declined to *two thirds* of the citywide rate. (3) While suicide was once four to five times more prevalent among Chinese American males than females, the ratio had steadily changed in recent years, with a growing incidence of Chinese American women committing suicide. (4) For both sexes, the most suicide-prone decade was between fifty-five and sixty-five years of age. The mean age for men had been progressively decreasing. (5) Consistent with citywide trends, barbiturate overdose had become the most frequent mode of suicide, although among Chinese American women hanging is more common. Firearms had not been used by Chinese American males in a single case since 1965. (6) Suicide in the Chinese American male was most often imputed to despondency over poor physical health, whereas the Chinese American female typically suffered interpersonal conflicts and sometimes had a history of identified psychiatric disorders.

Bourne's report is probably the most detailed on Chinese Americans to date. His findings, however, are difficult to reconcile with those of Sung. Since Sung did not mention the source of her data or the period of time covered by her analysis, it is not possible to analyze the discrepancy between the two studies. Even more interesting are the different interpretations provided by Sung and Hsu on the ways that Chinese Americans deal with unhappiness. For Sung, unhappiness is turned inward to the self. According to Hsu, unhappiness is turned "outward" and shared by relatives and friends.

Kalish's (1968) data on the Chinese Americans in the state of Hawaii add to the confusion. Looking at the suicide rate from 1959 to 1965, he found that Chinese Americans had only a slightly lower rate than that of Caucasians, a finding that is inconsistent with Hsu's data. It is not clear why the statistics on Chinese American suicides are so discrepant. Sampling differences, calculations from different time periods, geographical differences, and the use of different sources of data may account for some of the inconsistencies in the various studies. However, if rates or reports of rates fluctuate so greatly, then generalizations concerning suicide among Chinese Americans are impossible to make with any degree of confidence. Alcantara (1977) has also noted discrepancies in the reporting of suicide rates among Pilipino Americans in Hawaii. Incidentally, reports of rates among other Asian American groups are difficult to find. Kalish's study did reveal that Hawaiian Americans had a higher rate and that Japanese, part-Hawaiian, and Pilipino

American groups had lower rates than those of Caucasian Americans.

Juvenile Delinquency and Crime. Several individuals have commented on the extremely low rates of crime and juvenile delinquency among Chinese and Japanese Americans (Abbott and Abbott, 1968; Kitano, 1976; Petersen, 1978; Sung, 1967). Citing statistics from the Federal Bureau of Investigation, Kitano reported the following arrest rates for different groups per 100,000: Whites, 613; Blacks, 1,641; American Indians, 1,719; Chinese Americans, 164; and Japanese Americans, 264. Petersen believes that the low recorded rates of crime and delinquency for these two Asian American groups are valid, although he acknowledges that criminal acts in Chinatowns are underreported.

A great deal of recent interest has focused on youth gangs in various Chinatowns throughout the nation. Although the existence of such gangs is not a recent phenomenon, gang activities and overt violence have increased. Gang wars, murders, extortion, and robberies have caused many restaurants and shops in the Chinatowns of San Francisco and New York to close their doors early in the evening. Lyman (1977) attributes the increased formation of gangs to (1) an increase in the number of youths, particularly immigrants; (2) frustration over racism and powerlessness; (3) inability to succeed in school because of English-language problems and culture conflicts; and (4) the financial gains obtained through gang activities. Whereas the American born or those with some college education share many of the same frustrations as gang members, their activities are often channeled into social and political protest. For youths in gangs, the avenues for success in the social system (for example, education and occupational mobility) are more limited. Participation in gangs may mean financial rewards, feelings of power, camaraderie with other members, and status (Sung, 1979).

According to Sung (1979), several tongs (Chinese associations) hired gangs to protect illegal gambling activities. However, gang members intimidated the tongs as well as Chinese American businesses. They often forced merchants to pay for protection and even robbed the merchants, who were fearful of reporting the crimes to the police. Violence also increased because of competition among different gangs. Individuals are recruited as gang members, either by the lure of gang activities or by threats (in which case gang members often identify prospective members who may be having trouble in school and who are physically fit and then use strong-arm tactics to force the youths into the gang).

Although little is actually known about crime and delinquency among Chinese and Japanese Americans, even less is known about the situation of other Asian American groups. In Hawaii Samoan and Pilipino Americans are stereotyped as being more prone to violence and crime than other Asian Americans. The relatively recent immigration of these groups, the limits on social and economic mobility, and the unique cultural conflicts experienced by these groups may partially explain the higher rates of crime. However, until more data are available, we are hesitant to make generalizations.

Summary

We began this chapter by posing a major question: Are there specific kinds of mental health problems encountered by Asian Americans? In order to examine this question, we attempted to determine whether there are differences in the expression of symptoms. Most studies reveal that cultural factors do influence the expression of symptoms. For Asian Americans, psychological distress is often accompanied by somatic or physical problems. As to whether Asian Americans show differences from Caucasian Americans in the distribution of disorders, we indicated that this issue cannot be resolved because of the lack of research and the methodological problems involved in such research.

Finally, brief descriptions were provided of high-risk groups (the elderly, wives of United States servicemen, Eurasians, Indochinese, and Pacific Island Americans) and specific areas of mental health problems (alcohol consumption, drug abuse, suicide, and juvenile delinquency and crime). The discussions were not intended to be inclusive of all high-risk groups or of all specific areas of disturbance (for example, there is growing concern over specific problems, such as developmentally disabled Asian Americans, as noted by Lim-Yee and Gee in a personal communication, September 12, 1980); however, they do reflect the diverse and complicated problems facing Asian Americans—problems that need more research and attention. To better understand these problems and mental health issues, we now turn to a discussion of family and culture. Family and culture are the means by which individuals develop skills in adjusting, adapting, interpreting, and negotiating with the environment.

4

Understanding the Asian American Family

Social scientists who examine Asian and Pacific American groups invariably discuss the significance of the family and kinship systems. The importance of the family has been stressed for Chinese Americans (Lyman, 1974; Tseng and Char, 1974; Weiss, 1974), Japanese Americans (Kitano and Kikumura, 1976; Petersen, 1978), Korean Americans (B. L. C. Kim, 1980), Pilipino Americans (Morales, 1974; Ponce, 1974), Samoan Americans (Markoff and Bond, 1974; Shu and Satele, 1977), and Vietnamese Americans (Aylesworth, Ossorio, and Osaki, 1980). Shon (1980a, pp. 725-726) notes that "The family plays a very important role in most AAPA [Asian and Pacific American] cultures, unlike in American society where family bonds are much looser and one thinks primarily of the nuclear family of parents and children. In American society the individual breaks away from the family to go his own way. The ideals of individuality, independence, and self-sufficiency are stressed by society. . . . However, the tradition of most Asian and Pacific American cultures tends to place a great emphasis on the family as the central unit rather than the individual."

What role does the family play in facilitating mental health? How valid are conceptualizations of particular Asian families? What is the impact on the family of living in a multicultural society? These are the major questions addressed in this chapter. Traditionally, certain aspects of Asian and Asian American families have been romanticized and have been proposed as enhancing adjustment and well-being. Without resorting to romanticism, we want to sift out characteristics of certain Asian American families that may facilitate as well as hinder adaptation. There are strengths and costs inherent in one's family and culture, and the ultimate value of family and culture cannot be assessed independently of the individual's total (for example, multicultural) environment. As a starting point for our discussion, the views of Hsu on the Chinese and DeVos on the Japanese American are presented.

Hsu's Theory

Francis Hsu, past president of the American Anthropological Association, has been one of the major forces in defining Chinese family and culture. Two features are apparent in Hsu's theory of Chinese culture. First, he believes that Chinese culture can be defined and contrasted with Western culture; that is, he believes that it is meaningful to contrast different cultures and values, despite individual differences. Second, he uses cultural contrasts to develop a theory of human beings that is intended to have universal applicability.

Hsu (1971) essentially believes that all human beings behave according to certain roles or rules in interpersonal relationships (for example, a teacher, husband, nurse, and political leader learn certain ways of acting as a function of the role assumed) and according to an affective need for social and emotional intimacy that makes life meaningful. Most individuals develop affective and social bonds with immediate members of the family, such as parents, siblings, or other close relatives. Chinese culture stresses that these bonds should be continuous, so that the individual's self-esteem and future are tied to the family or kin. The family remains as an important root for the individual throughout the person's lifetime, even if that person leaves for another country and is isolated from the family. Western culture, with its emphasis on rugged individualism, pushes the person to find his or her own roots away from the affectionate and intimate bonds first learned in the family. While having greater freedom and independence, the individual who is socialized in Western culture begins to lose the affective bonds that define human existence. Therefore, the individualistic person is forced to find meaning by (1) self-exploration and an existential search for meaning or (2) a search for material goals or social, religious, or political causes in an attempt to satisfy the affective needs. Affective relationships with peers are difficult, since socialization to values of individualism fosters a great deal of competition. Chinese culture, on the other hand, emphasizes kinship from birth to death, so that affective or emotional needs tend to be fulfilled at the price of conformity to family and elders.

These cultural differences can also be seen in our techniques of social control. For example, in attempting to stop air piracy (skyjackings), we have used detection devices (electronic hardware, passenger searches, personality profile analyses of suspected skyjackers, and so on), force (sky marshals), or the elimination of sanctuaries for hijacked planes; in drug abuse we try to detect and punish pushers and to explain the disastrous effects of drugs to youths; in keeping children from opening medicine bottles, we have invented child-proof lids that can be opened only by complicated maneuvers, often sacrificing our fingernails in the process; to see that fewer people are killed in auto accidents, we have devised an intricate system whereby cars emit an irritating noise or will not start unless seat belts are fastened. All these measures are culturally determined and involve external restraints. For many Asian Americans, restraints are more internalized according to family values, so that arousing feelings of guilt or shame can act as a powerful means of social control. Hsu (1973) feels that in our society we have failed to emphasize why people want to hijack planes, why youths are "turning on" to drugs, why children attempt to open medicine bottles despite warnings from parents, and why individuals are so little concerned with highway safety. In an individual-centered society, people do their "own thing." Achievements as well as failures are attributed to the individual. Similarly, techniques of social control are externally applied to restrain individual dispositions. Hsu indicates that an individual-centered Western model of human beings cannot provide a meaningful analysis and resolution of social ills. In essence, he proposes that solutions to social problems are superficial when generated from an individual-centered model, which is limited in its ability to conceptualize human beings. To better understand Hsu's criticisms, it is necessary to examine his sociocentric model of human beings.

A Sociocentric Model. Hsu (1971, 1973) believes that a more precise conceptualization of human beings as social and cultural beings is needed. He posits eight "layers" (7 to 0) that are relevant in understanding human beings.

Layers 7 and 6 consist of the "unconscious" and "preconscious" and correspond to Freudian or classical psychoanalytic notions. Psychic materials in these layers are repressed or semirepressed. Although they influence behaviors, these two layers (in contrast to a psychoanalytic approach) are not important determinants of personality.

Layer 5, the "unexpressed conscious," contains material that is generally kept private by the individual. This material is not communicated to others because the person (1) is afraid to communicate it, (2) feels that others will not understand or care, (3) believes that it is difficult to verbalize, or (4) is ashamed to divulge it.

Layer 4, termed the "expressible conscious," contains ideas and feelings—such as love, greed, vision, hatred, fear, and knowledge—which the individual can and does communicate to others, who in turn understand and respond to the communication.

Ideas, humans, gods, and things that comprise the individual's intimate society and culture are included in Layer 3. The person has an intimate relationship with the contents of this layer—a relationship based more on feelings (affect) than on functional usefulness. Significant others (for example, parents, siblings, and spouse) are likely to be included in Layer 3. Cherished pets and ideals can also be included. For example, Hsu believes that for many Americans the idea of privacy is part of Layer 3. Jesus is for most Christians, but Buddha is not; bedroom furniture may be, but park benches are not. One's sentimental attachment to a gift may be. The departure of, or infringement on, persons, ideas, or things in Layer 3 is likely to cause emotional problems. The death of a significant other, the loss of a sentimental object, and challenges from others of one's cherished principles will cause turmoil in the individual. For Hsu, this layer is centrally important in personality.

Layer 2 consists of humans to whom one relates by roles. The relationship is based on usefulness rather than feeling or affect. For example, a store clerk acts out a role and must have customers; a teacher must have students; a physician must have patients; a secretary must have an employer. These roles do not demand or imply intimacy. Loss of items in Layer 2 (such as the death of a student for a teacher) may not mean emotional turmoil, since attachments are based on roles. Cultural rules and artifacts can also be a part of Layer 2. Traffic rules and ways of negotiating define roles but are not usually performed with a great deal of emotional attachment. Hsu admits that in different societies, and for different persons, the contents of layers can vary. However, he maintains that layer distinctions themselves are important.

Layer 1 contains people, gods, ideas, and things that exist as a part of one's culture but apart from oneself. In our society an agnostic has little to do with churches. Many Americans have little knowledge of or contact with members of the ethnic minorities.

Peoples, customs, and things that are not even nominally a part of one are included in Layer 0. Whereas an individual may be exposed to the contents of Layer 1 (for instance, an individual having no previous contact with ethnic minority groups may go to a large university with an ethnically diverse student body), he or she may never have contact with items in Layer 0. Examples of items in Layer 0 for many Americans may be the Great Wall of China or the people in Bolivia.

Implications for Adjustment. Hsu's theory is one that (1)

appreciates intrapsychic as well as social and external phenomena; (2) considers the dimensions of intimacy, role behavior, and familiarity; and (3) classes individual ideas, rules, and things. He believes that every individual needs the affective relationships of Layer 3, since they define human existence and provide a sense of well-being. Loss of affective relationships (through the death of a loved one, violation of a cherished idea or belief, and so forth) can cause emotional trauma, diminished interest in life, or mental disorders. To maintain mental health, the theory assumes, one should develop Layer 3 rather than other layers. Furthermore, to satisfy the affective need for intimacy, one should cultivate human beings over nonhuman beings or objects.

Individuals tend to maintain a satisfactory level of psychic and interpersonal equilibrium or psychosocial homeostasis. Normally, the main psychic source for action and for communication with others comes from Layer 4. Layers 6 and 7 cannot be consciously used, since the contents are largely repressed and idiosyncratic; Layer 5 cannot be mobilized because of the interpersonal tensions created by its contents. The lack of affective attachments to items in Layers 2, 1, and 0 makes it difficult to use the items in satisfying affective needs. The key to understanding human beings, culture, response to stress, self-esteem, and the use of interpersonal resources lies in Layer 3. It is this layer that must be satisfied and fulfilled.

Hsu notes that some cultures make it easier to fulfill the affective and intimate needs of Layer 3. In Chinese culture parents and kin are included in Layer 3. They share the individual's triumphs and failures; they provide a sense of continuity and belongingness. Thus, a person's self-esteem and identity are tied to kinship. The permanence of these ties means that Chinese are able to feel continued levels of intimacy and affect with significant others. There is no strong need to develop other layers, since the network of intimacy is available. Even when the Chinese individual moves away from family (as the early immigrants from China did), kinship (family associations) or locality (district associations) ties were quickly developed. In the family children are socialized to a network whereby filial piety and deference to elders are stressed. Child rights are not emphasized, and children are often raised by parents, grandparents, and other relatives rather than by the parents alone.

The individualistic person has a more difficult time achieving psychosocial homeostasis. The individual must try to seek items from other layers to incorporate into Layer 3. For instance, an existential search for identity and selfhood may represent an attempt to incorporate items from Layers 6 and 7 into Layer 3; by finding meaning in acquiring wealth, in political revolutions, in missionary conquests, the individual pulls contents from Layers 2, 1, and 0 into Layer 3. In Hsu's view, Western individuals often use "substitutes" to satisfy affective needs.

The implications for mental health are clear. Many of the social ills seen in American society can be attributed to unsatisfied affective needs; the development of affective ties and family relationships is the key to resolving societal problems. The family is perceived as a major resource in providing stability, a sense of self-esteem, and satisfaction. The strength in Chinese culture is the family and kinship networks.

Critical Evaluation. Hsu's ideas are rich, intriguing, and refreshing. His cultural contrasts are insightful, and he presents powerful anecdotes and examples to illustrate his points. However, questions can be raised concerning (1) the theory itself, (2) the cultural contrasts, and (3) the identified strengths of Chinese families. With respect to the theory advanced by Hsu, at least two points are important. First, a major assumption is that human beings have an essential need for intimacy and affective relationships with others. This notion is difficult to test, although many social scientists would probably not disagree with it. Second, the theory assumes that the affective need can be best satisfied by other human beings and that, in the absence of—and as a substitute for—intimate relationships with others, the person will seek intimate relationships with political causes, gods, or things. But surely one can have satisfactory levels of intimacy with others and yet pursue political causes and things. Moreover, the incorporation of non-Layer-3 contents into Layer 3 may not always imply a deficiency in Layer 3. Even if we were to accept Hsu's arguments that Chinese are more family oriented than Westerners, who are more individualistic, and that Chinese have traditionally not incorporated political causes, gods, or things in their intimate or personal affective levels, cause and effect are difficult to determine. An alternative explanation is that if one is devoted and committed to the family, one simply has less time to become involved with political causes and other issues. Another possibility is that Chinese cultural values may discourage involvement and interests in areas outside the family (Layer 3). The issue is whether it is necessary to propose a psychosocial homeostasis model in order to account for human behavior. In all fairness, Hsu himself felt that hypotheses from his theory should be tested. At this point the theory is a grand design supported by Hsu's observations, as was the case with Freud's construction of his psychoanalytic theory.

With respect to the cultural contrasts, Hsu's idea that Chinese are less likely to become involved in political causes, missionary ventures, acquisition of wealth, and so on, may be questioned, since his beliefs are based primarily on observational techniques rather than empirical evidence.

Finally, Hsu believes that one strength in Chinese mental health is that family ties enable the individual to share problems, to have affective needs satisfied, and to have a sense of belongingness and continuity. Certainly, these are desirable characteristics. However, strong kinship ties can also cause major problems for the person. Implicit in the strong relationship is the need to conform to parents or elders. That is, there is a price paid—namely, the necessity to obey elders. One must suppress individual inclinations or risk the disruption of family ties. For example, if one wishes to pursue a career disapproved by one's parents, individual wants and needs must be denied if family harmony is to be maintained. A related problem is that while culturally and structurally one is pressured to relate to family and kin, much conflict may exist within families. The following case involving one of the authors illustrates this point:

> At the advice of a close friend, Mae C. decided to seek services at a mental health center. She was extremely distraught and tearful as she related her dilemma. An im-

migrant from Hong Kong several years ago, Mae met and married her husband (also a recent immigrant from Hong Kong). Their marriage was apparently going fairly well until six months ago, when her husband succeeded in bringing over his parents from Hong Kong. While not enthusiastic about having her parents-in-law live with her, Mae realized that her husband wanted them and that both she and her husband were obligated to help their parents (her own parents were still in Hong Kong).

After the parents arrived, Mae found that she was expected to serve them. For example, the mother-in-law would expect Mae to cook and serve dinner, to wash all the clothes, and to do other chores. At the same time, she would constantly complain that Mae did not cook the dinner right, that the house was always messy, and that Mae should wash certain clothes separately. The parents-in-law also displaced Mae and her husband from the master bedroom. The guest room was located in the basement, and the parents refused to sleep in the basement because it reminded them of a tomb.

Mae would occasionally complain to her husband about his parents. The husband would excuse his parents' demands by indicating, "They are my parents and they're getting old." In general, he avoided any potential conflict; if he took sides, he supported his parents. Although Mae realized that she had an obligation to his parents, the situation was becoming intolerable to her.

What kind of solution can be found in Mae's case? We could have encouraged Mae to confront her in-laws. We could have invited Mae and her husband to come in for family therapy and then have them work with the parents. However, in Mae's particular case, such tactics would have been difficult for her or her husband to carry out. Feelings of guilt and shame would have been extensive, and family relationships would have been seriously jeopardized. We did find that Mae considered one relative, her uncle (the older brother of the mother-in-law), to be quite understanding and sensitive. We suggested that she contact the uncle, who lived in a city about fifty miles from Mae. The uncle, realizing the gravity of the situation, visited Mae and her family. After having dinner with the family, he took his sister aside and told her that Mae looked very unhappy, that possibly she was working too hard, and that she needed a little more praise for the work that she was doing in taking care of everyone. The mother-in-law expressed surprise over Mae's unhappiness and agreed that Mae was doing a fine job. Without directly confronting each other, Mae's uncle and mother-in-law understood the subtle messages each conveyed. After this interaction Mae reported that her mother-in-law's criticisms did noticeably diminish and that she had even begun to help Mae with the chores.

Obviously, not all family relationships involve such conflicts. However, the role obligations between Mae and her husband, Mae and her parents-in-law, and her husband and his parents made it difficult for Mae to find a solution to the demands and complaints of her parents-in-law.

Another problem is that individuals with strong family ties suffer extreme shame or guilt if they fail to achieve what their families expect them to achieve or if they violate family rules of conduct. Pressures from parents for their children to work hard, to achieve, and to be successful have resulted in high educational and occupational achievements among many Chinese Americans. Such pressures may also disturb one's emotional well-being. Having internalized values in high achievement, an individual may be constantly self-critical and dissatisfied despite relatively high levels of success. Moreover, persons who perform in a mediocre manner or who fail to achieve may feel a deep sense of shame or alienation.

Thus, although the family and kinship system does satisfy affective needs and provide a sense of continuity and belongingness, there are costs associated with the family structure. Three important factors must be considered when one analyzes the role of family in mental health. First, some determination must be made of the areas where mental health strengths and costs are reflected. Universal or absolute views of the positive or negative nature of families are inappropriate. Psychological well-being may be enhanced in some areas but limited in other areas because of one's family structure. Second, and consistent with our emphasis on the importance of person-environment matches, the role of the family in adaptation cannot be assessed independently of person-environment interactions. To the extent that the family facilitates person-environment matches, the family serves a valuable function. The issue concerns the degree to which Chinese cultural values and family structure serve Chinese living in the United States. If the family helps one to adapt in this environment, then it has strengths. If it does not, then the family is not transmitting functional skills. Third, we again stress the enormous variability in Chinese American families. Not all families stress achievement; not all families and relatives feel a sense of togetherness or mutual obligation.

DeVos's Theory

In contrast to the significance of affective relationships in Hsu's theory, DeVos adopts the position that role and structure within the Japanese American family are responsible for the individual's ability to adapt and adjust. DeVos (1978) argues that Japanese Americans have succeeded in the sense that they have relatively high levels of academic achievement and income and low rates of juvenile delinquency, mental disorders, and alcoholism. He addresses the question of why Japanese Americans have fared so well despite minority group status and discrimination in American society. DeVos's theory is based on the notion that role playing within the Japanese American family protects individuals from "social diseases."

Family Roles. In DeVos's view, Americans tend to relate to each other in an intimate fashion without resorting to the playing of roles. "Be yourself," "Be open and honest," "Don't be phony," and "Don't play roles or games" are advocated in American society. In the Japanese tradition, however, "being oneself" is subordinate to acting in accordance with role expectations; and members of a family (for example, father, mother, eldest child, son, and daughter) have clearly defined roles. For the Japanese, the "sincere" individual acts in accordance with role expectations, not personal subjective feelings. Americans would view such a person as insincere, since, for Americans, a sincere person behaves on the basis of openness and feelings rather than role prescriptions.

The role of the Japanese father is to be the head of the household. This role is irreproachably legitimate and dominant, demanding unquestioned respect from the child. The mother is expected to be deferent to and supportive of her husband. In playing her role as mother, she sees to it that her children develop a proper attitude toward their father. She demonstrates self-control and avoids direct confrontation. Children growing up in these families are socialized to these role-appropriate male-female, husband-wife, father-mother, and parent-child relationships.

DeVos sees two important consequences of the role structure in Japanese American families. First, males who suffer humiliation or who experience racial discrimination in the outside world can still return to an intact family where they are not degraded. Because of the role structure, the father still maintains head-of-household status, and personal inadequacies or humiliations suffered elsewhere are not echoed within the family. Thus, the family provides support and protection. When family roles deteriorate (for instance, when wives criticize husbands, which often results in children's adopting a negative attitude toward their fathers), fathers frequently become quite deviant. Second, although the role structure creates stability and security, it can also cause problems. For example, to portray the father role, a father may avoid self-disclosure, personal feelings, and expressions of affection; as a result, an emotional distance is created between father and children. In fact, many Japanese American children complain that there is much distance between themselves and their fathers.

It is interesting to compare the social scientist view of DeVos with that of Jeanne Wakatsuki Houston, a writer. Having coauthored *Farewell to Manzanar,* a personal account of her family's experiences during and after World War II, Houston (1980), in a more recent article, poignantly describes the family's relationships and her perspective of womanhood:

> There was no question in my mind that my mother loved my father; that is why she served him. This attitude,

that to serve meant to love, became an integral part of my psychological makeup and a source of confusion when I later began to relate to men.

There was also no question in my mind that my father was absolute authority in their relationship and in his relationship to his children. During and after the Second World War, when his dreams and economic situation had hit bottom, and he was too old to start over again as he had already done several times, he raged at his wife and family and drank. His frustration toward the society that rejected and humiliated him caused him to turn on his own and on himself. I never understood how she so patiently endured him during those times. But she never abandoned him, understanding, as I did not, the reasons for his anguish, for his sense of failure.

Even though respect for him diminished then, I always felt that he was very powerful and that he dominated her with this power. As they grew older and inevitable thoughts of their passing entered my mind, I worried that she would be lost if he died before her. When that sad day arrived, I learned what is meant by the Asian philosophical truism "Softness is strength." I had taken my gravely ill father, along with my mother, to see his doctor. The doctor informed me privately that we should take him to the hospital where he would be comfortable, as he could not live more than ten days.

It was raining. I numbly drove the car toward the hospital, straining to see through the blurred windshield and my own tears. My mother was not crying. "Riku," he said, weakly. He never called her Riku . . . always "Mama." "Don't leave me. Stay with me at the hospital. They won't know how to cook for me . . . or how to care for me." She patted his hand. "You've been a good wife. You've always been the strong one."

Not wanting him to tire, I tried to quiet him. He sat up bolt-like and roared like a lion. "Shut up!" I quaked at his forcefulness, but felt some comfort in knowing he could still "save face" and be the final authority to his children, even at death's door. My mother's quiet strength filled the car as she gently stroked his forehead. Without tears or panic she assured him she would stay with him until the end.

He died that afternoon a few hours after he entered the hospital. For the ten years afterward that my mother lived, she never once appeared lost or rudderless, as I feared she would be with him gone. Hadn't he been the center of her life? Hadn't the forms in their relationship, the rituals of their roles all affirmed his power over her? No. She had been the strong one. The structure had been created for him; but it was her essence that has sustained it [p. 20; Copyright 1980 by Science and Behavior Books].

Houston's recollections seem to support DeVos's analysis of the Japanese American family. She acknowledges her father's authority and dominance, her mother's supportive role, and the well-structured family relationships. Her father's humiliations and frustrations in American society during the era of World War II were buffered by her mother. However, Houston tends to emphasize her mother's strength as a patient, caring, understanding, and supportive person. She implies that the role of wife and mother, though overtly subordinate to that of husband and father, is actually not one of subservience or inferiority. Moreover, Houston does not seem to view role playing as a process devoid of affect, where roles are assumed because of duty and obligation. In her family the enactment of roles meant love.

Critical Evaluation. DeVos believes that Japanese Americans have succeeded rather well in American society. He attributes the success to the quality of family interactions, where stability in role playing provides security in maintaining self-esteem. One serious problem in his analysis is the assertion of Japanese American success and lack of "social diseases." As indicated in Chapter Two, Japanese Americans do experience significant mental health problems, and the rates of mental disturbance have been considerably underestimated. In making his assertion, DeVos relies on the low incidence of Japanese Americans treated for mental disturbance. However, we cannot state with any degree of confidence whether the rates are higher, lower, or similar in comparison to those of other Americans. DeVos himself is aware of the psychological stress experienced by Japanese Americans as members of a physically identifiable minority group and by youths who feel some degree of distance between themselves and their "traditional" fathers.

With respect to education, income, and occupational mobility, there is evidence that Japanese Americans have made major achievements. For example, Sue, Sue, and Sue (1975) note that in 1970 the median family income ($12,515) and median level of education (12.5 years) for Japanese Americans were higher than the income ($9,590) and educational levels (12.1 years) for the rest of the United States population. They are quick to add, however, that a case can be built for viewing Japanese Americans as a group that continues to suffer from prejudice and discrimination. In other words, success is a blanket concept that fails to convey the various factors that comprise it. Our concern is over the description of Japanese Americans as a model minority group and the "halo effect" that frequently accompanies discussion of this group.

DeVos's analysis seems to downplay emotional aspects and mutual influence in interaction patterns. As mentioned by Houston, roles are played in the family, but such roles are not devoid of emotion. Moreover, the mother may exert considerable influence on the father without directly undermining the father's role. Japanese American family interactions contain attempts at social influence and control, but in an indirect manner rather than in the form of confrontive statements. Instead of urging her husband to "hurry up" because they are late in leaving for a dinner party, for example, the wife may suggest to her husband that they should leave quickly by saying, "It's beginning to rain very hard and the traffic should be very busy" (the implication is that driving to the party will require a great deal of time). Rather than telling a child to study instead of watching television, a parent may say, "I bet Linda (a close Japanese American friend of the child) is studying right now" or "That television program seems to be really boring." Such indirect techniques can lead to confusion and misinterpretations, but they avoid direct attacks that often result in irreconcilable differences and a loss of face (Kitano and Kikumura, 1976).

Research on Families

Although many social scientists have discussed various Asian and Pacific American families, there have been few empirical studies of family dynamics or of childrearing practices, particularly for groups other than Chinese and Japanese Americans. The available research investigations have been of two major types: (1) comparisons of changing attitudes on family practices because of assimilation and (2) ethnic differences in childrearing practices. For example, Connor (1974b) studied three different generations (Issei, Nisei, and Sansei) of Japanese Americans and found that the later generations of American-born Japanese had less of a sense of Japanese identity and respect for the family name and Japanese community. Similarly, Kitano (1961, 1964), using the Parental Attitude Research Inventory (PARI), found that older generations of Japanese American women were more restrictive and traditionally Japanese in their childrearing attitudes than more recent generations of Japanese Americans. Young (1972a, 1972b) investigated family patterns among foreign-born and Hawaii-born Chinese Americans. Although acknowledging the impact of assimilation, she found many common attitudes between immigrant and American-born Chinese. Both groups believed in the crucial role of education and hard work in success, the importance of family needs over individual desires, and the value of delayed gratification. Nevertheless, the value of the extended family, considered important in China, was superseded by the nuclear family in the Hawaii-born group.

By examining the attitudes and practices in the families of various groups, one can gain insight into ethnic differences. Osako (1976) found that, on behavioral and attitudinal measures, Japanese Americans showed greater relatedness with their parents than Caucasian Americans did. Specifically, Japanese Americans tended to live closer, to express higher levels of obligation, to provide more financial assistance, and to interact more frequently with their parents. Chinese American mothers are more restrictive in their childrearing practices than Jewish and Protestant mothers, as measured by the PARI (Kriger and Kroes, 1972). Sollenberger (1968) compared New York China-town mothers with a non–Chinese American sample in the Cambridge, Massachusetts area. Results indicated that the Chinese American mothers were more likely to discourage physical aggression, demand conformity, provide nurturance and protection, expect filial duties, and anticipate high educational achievements in their children. In an analysis of mother-child interaction patterns in Chinese, Mexican, and Caucasian Americans, Steward and Steward (1973) concluded that Chinese American mothers used feedback and statements rather than posing questions in teaching their children, who exhibited a great deal of deference to their mothers.

Most of the findings from these studies do not contradict the descriptions of the family as implied in the analyses of Hsu and of DeVos. Achievement orientation, the closeness and importance of the family, conformity, and the like, are characteristics consistent with those advanced by both Hsu and DeVos.

Implications for Mental Health

It is somewhat difficult to draw implications for mental health for Asian and Pacific Americans, since family theories and research have focused for the most part on Chinese and Japanese Americans. However, it is probably safe to say that most Asian and Pacific American families do share general cultural characteristics, such as close family ties, conformity within the family, role structures, and filial piety. With these characteristics in mind, do Asian and Pacific American families foster greater mental health than Western or Caucasian American families do?

Hsu and DeVos both seem to answer this question affirmatively, although for different reasons. Hsu believes that Chinese American families are better able to satisfy a basic need for interpersonal intimacy and to provide social support. DeVos contends that the integrity of Japanese American family roles and structure defends against the impact of stress. Yet, as we have indicated, the family structure may generate intense conflicts; furthermore, reports of the success and well-being of Asian/Pacific Americans have been overrated.

From our perspective, the importance of the family in promoting mental health depends on at least two major considerations: the structure and content of families and the transmission of adaptive skills in confronting one's environment. In regard to structure, Hsu is probably correct in asserting that some cultures are better able to meet affective interpersonal needs of individuals; and DeVos is probably correct in asserting that set roles in the family provide stability, order, predictability, and security—and therefore tend to promote mental health. Seligman (1975) indicates that order and predictability in relationships are related to psychological well-being; and Dohrenwend and Dohrenwend (1974b) note that rapid life changes, such as disruptions in family relationships, can act as stressors.

In addition to structural aspects of families, content is also important. By content, we mean the nature of family relationships. The case of Mae C., presented earlier, illustrates that family obligations can hinder resolution of interpersonal conflicts (although in Mae's case a solution was found). The very closeness of family relationships may create extraordinary problems involving individual desires versus family obligations. A person may want to behave in accordance with his or her own desires and needs rather than in accordance with parental dictates. Allegiances with various family members may be split. For example, husbands and wives frequently give financial assistance to their parents. What happens if, for example, the husband feels obligated to contribute financially to his parents when his own nuclear family needs the money? Osako (1976) found that one major conflict among Nisei Japanese Americans was the need to make sacrifices in order to support their parents, although the majority of the Nisei reported that funding for their children's education took precedence over assistance to parents. Another potential problem stems from family expectations. Young's (1972a) research has shown that Chinese American parents expect and often demand high levels of educational and occupational achievement. Kim (1980) has also found that immigrant Korean American parents have high educational expectations and standards for their children. Indeed, many Asian and Pacific American families press family members for high levels of performance. Such demands for achievement, while acting as a strong motivator for performance, may result not only in high achievement levels but also in psychological costs involving continual dissatisfaction over one's level of performance. We have encountered many students with distinguished academic records who feel that their parents offer little praise for their accomplishments, preferring to emphasize that the students can still do better. Finally, the strong role structures defined in the family do sometimes create emotional distance, as noted by DeVos (1978) in the relationship between fathers and children.

In assessing the role of family in mental health, one also must consider the family's ability to prepare individuals to adapt to the demands of the external environment. If the values and behaviors that are acquired in an ethnic minority or subcultural group are not functional in the larger groups or society, then adjustment is not facilitated. What cultural or familial aspects can be considered strengths or weaknesses in Asian and Pacific American families? For several reasons this question is difficult to answer. First, culture is not static. Particularly in the United States, where there are many different cultural groups and where there is much within-group diversity, it is not possible to say exactly what constitutes an Asian culture, an Asian American culture, or an American culture. Second, the attitudes and behaviors encouraged in one's subcultural groups may directly conflict with those encouraged by the larger society. Therefore, how does one go about assessing strengths and weaknesses in the family? In evaluating the role of Asian and Pacific Islander American families in the United States, we will consider here the areas of culture conflict, racism, and social change.

Culture Conflict. Culture conflict occurs whenever (1) members of one culture come into prolonged and close contact with the norms, values, and behavioral patterns of another culture; (2) the two cultures significantly differ from each other; and (3) conformance to each culture is rewarded and socialized. For Asian and Pacific American groups, all these conditions appear to be satisfied (see Sue and Chin, 1982). Contact can be assessed by its effects. That is, progressive assimilation and acculturation would be expected if contact occurs. As indicated by Fong (1965) and by Matsumoto, Meredith, and Masuda (1970), Asian and Pacific Americans whose families have been in the United States for several generations, who live outside an ethnic community, and who have American citizenship status are more acculturated to American society than are those whose families have not been here as long, who live within an ethnic community, and who are not American citizens.

The other two conditions—namely, that the two cultures differ from each other and that conformance to each culture is rewarded—also exist. The analyses of Hsu and of DeVos as well as the research cited earlier point to cultural differences and the different socialization techniques between Asian/Pacific American groups and Westerners or more mainstream Caucasian Americans. In view of these differences, many social scientists feel that exposure to different cultural demands creates problems. After reviewing a case study of a Chinese American client, Sommers (1960) noted the difficulty that the client had in developing a stable identity because of culture conflict. Similarly, Bourne (1975) found that young Chinese American clients at a mental health clinic exhibited anxiety over the inability to reconcile their parental wishes concerning filial piety and conformance to the family with the roles and values of youths in the larger society. Males reported problems involving passivity in social relationships, feelings of social isolation, and pressures for academic achievement; females expressed guilt feelings or conflicts in their relationships with Caucasian males. These findings are similar to those of Weiss (1970), who concluded that the acculturation process can create intense conflicts. He believes that Chinese American females are more acculturated and have received less invidious stereotypes than males. Therefore, they find it easier to date Caucasians. Chinese American males, on the other hand, are under strong pressures to achieve academically and have less opportunity to learn adaptive social skills. Fong (1973) found that serious problems were generated because the American educational system, where children are taught to assert independence and autonomy, seemed to undermine parental authority at home.

Discrepancies in acculturation between parents and children can have detrimental effects. Kurokawa (1969) studied the relationship between acculturation and medically attended injuries or accidents for Chinese and Japanese American children in the Kaiser Medical Plan. Medical records were available for the analysis of injuries, while interviews of mothers were conducted in order to determine childrearing practices and the degree of acculturation. Three acculturation patterns emerged: acculturated children of acculturated mothers, acculturated children of nonacculturated mothers, and nonacculturated children of nonacculturated mothers. Results indicated that acculturated children were more likely than nonacculturated children to be independent and venturesome, which increased the probability of their being exposed to hazards and accidents. Furthermore, children with acculturation conflicts at home (that is, the acculturated children of nonacculturated parents) appeared to have a higher accident rate—possibly because the tension and conflict at home made these children unable to cope with the hazards they encountered.

As these findings suggest, exposure to a multicultural environment may cause value conflicts within a family and within an individual. Such conflicts often occur between parents and children. They may also be found among siblings (for example, the eldest child who is less acculturated than younger brothers or sisters) or among husband and wife (for example, a "liberated" woman who cannot tolerate the more traditional status accorded women by her husband). In dealing with such conflicts, families need to be somewhat flexible. As Sue and Chin (1982) note, flexibility may be achieved if families adopt bicultural perspectives and orientations to adjust to bicultural influences. For example, a Chinese American student might be encouraged to defer to family elders but to be assertive in the presence of Caucasian teachers. In this way, the family encourages appropriate behaviors in specific situations. There may also be a unique blend of certain Asian and American patterns. Some Chinese Americans may eat Chinese food for dinner and have apple pie for dessert. Young married couples may consider their own nuclear family as the most important relationship and yet maintain strong affective bonds to their parents. In other words, the family may adapt to the exposure to conflicting values by developing unique patterns involving bicultural orientations.

Racism. Without dwelling on the documentation of racism

toward Asian and Pacific Americans, we do want to note that they have been subjected to discriminatory laws in the past (Kim, 1978). A recent report by the U.S. Commission on Civil Rights (1980) indicates that Asian Americans are underrepresented in managerial and administrative occupations, although their representation in professional and technical positions is high. Furthermore, compared to other Americans in the same professional and managerial positions, Asian Americans have higher educational levels but receive less income. The U.S. Commission on Civil Rights concluded that, in contrast to popular stereotypes, Asian Americans are not a successful minority group, free from discriminatory practices. Asian Americans themselves have expressed feelings of discrimination. In a survey of Chinese Americans in Chinatown, San Francisco, Loo and Yu (1980) found that fully 90 percent of the respondents believed that Chinese Americans must perform better than Caucasian Americans in order to get ahead. Being "as good as" is not enough.

Experiences of prejudice and discrimination affect psychological well-being. For Albee (1980), racism acts as a stressor; and Kramer, Rosen, and Willis (1973) contend that racism is a major determinant of psychological disorders for ethnic minority groups. With respect to family roles, to the extent that families are able to help members to function in spite of racism, then adjustment is facilitated. DeVos (1978) has argued that the role structure of Japanese American families (and perhaps of other Asian/Pacific American families) is so strong that racism tends not to disrupt internal family dynamics. Even if we accept DeVos's assumption, the question of how members of the family deal with encounters of prejudice and discrimination outside the family is unanswered.

Families must somehow prepare members for the realities of prejudice and discrimination and yet instill a sense of self-esteem, stable self-identity, achievement, and mastery in one's environment. While racism is best addressed by societal changes, one's particular handling of this problem is often dependent on the values and skills learned in the family.

Social Change. Many Asian and Pacific American families

must also adapt to rapid social changes. Social change can be stressful when it is rapid and unexpected, requires extensive changes in one's life-style, and occurs faster than one's ability to find adjustive techniques and resources. Because the Asian American population is now largely an immigrant one, there are particular problems. First, immigrants are often unable to come with all of their family members. This means that family patterns are disrupted. Second, children tend to become acculturated more rapidly than their immigrant parents, which causes family conflicts. Third, rapid life changes can create physical and psychological problems. Holmes and Masuda (1974) have found that the accumulation of a large number of life changes over a short period of time is associated with lowered well-being, especially if the changes are undesirable (Dohrenwend and Dohrenwend, 1974b). Immigrants undoubtedly experience life changes. Being in a new country, changing diet and life-style, trying to find a job, and the like, are major life events that demand a great deal of social readjustment. Hinkle (1974) examined a group of China-born immigrants living in the United States. They had undergone considerable cultural and social changes and exhibited more problems and illnesses on medical and psychological tests than a comparable group of Americans. How a family deals with separation of its members, differential rates of assimilation within the family, and changes in life-styles are important issues to consider.

Summary

Social scientists have often concluded that Asian American families are exceedingly stable and intact. For Hsu, the family satisfies important affective needs in individuals. For DeVos, the strong role structures enhance stability and adjustment. Their belief is that such families promote mental health and achievement in American society. While there is research that supports the cohesiveness of certain Asian American families, our view is that the role of family patterns in facilitating the mental health of its members is complex. The very closeness and cohesiveness of family members may also create problems involving independence versus conformity or individualism versus group centeredness. The value of one's family background cannot be assessed independently of the environmental demands. For Asian and Pacific Americans, the problems of culture conflict, prejudice/discrimination, and social change create considerable stress.

5

Personality, Sex-Role Conflict, and Ethnic Identity

The effects of family upbringing, cultural values, and experiences with others can be seen in the personality patterns of people—in their characteristic behaviors and thoughts, unique pattern of traits, or dominant attributes. The area of personality has emerged as the most controversial one for Asian Americans. After Sue and Sue (1971) published a paper intended to stimulate discussion among Asian Americans, they unexpectedly created a dispute on Asian American personality, with heated replies and rejoinders from eight different social scientists over a period of five years. The controversy dealt with the issue of how best to conceptualize Asian American personality. Related issues, such as sex roles, stereotypes, and individual and group identity, also have aroused strong emotional reactions.

The Personality Controversy

During the late 1960s, a number of Asian American studies programs were established on university campuses. A direct result of student activism and civil rights efforts, these programs were intended, among other things, to provide a more accurate portrayal of Asian American experiences and to combat racism (Endo, 1973). An alliance between such groups as Chinese, Japanese, Korean, and Philipino Americans under the rubric "Asian Americans" was at the time new and strange. It signified a stronger unification of groups that heretofore had only loosely joined together because of similar ethnic experiences. The self-designation of "Asian American" rather than "Oriental American" symbolized a political stance concerning self-definition and self-determination among Asian American groups. The student movement was joined by many others—the elderly, professionals, politicians, the indigent, and recent immigrants—who wanted to attack racism and to develop a stronger consciousness of ethnic identity as Asian Americans in the United States.

It was against this background that Sue and Sue (1971) developed their views of Asian American personality. (More accurately, their analysis was specifically of Chinese American personality although it was intended to be applicable to Asian Americans in general.) Traditionally, personality was considered a function of American or Western culture and the particular Asian culture. Therefore, Asian Americans could be placed on a dimension ranging from unacculturated (predominantly Asian) to acculturated (or "Americanized"). The Sues wanted to consider not only Asian and American cultures but also racism as factors that influenced personality. They developed a typological scheme to describe what they saw as three "types" of Asian Americans. The first type, the "traditionalist," strongly internalizes Asian values. Traditionalists identify with their particular culture and conform to parental wishes concerning filial piety and high achievement in order to bring a good name to the family. They tend to prefer socializing with members of their own ethnic group. The second type, the "marginal" individual, desires assimilation, rejects ethnic values, and often exhibits racial self-hatred. Marginal individuals tend to associate with Caucasian Americans and are at the opposite end of the acculturation/assimilation dimension from traditionalists. The Sues' third type, the "Asian American," cannot be easily placed on the acculturation/assimilation continuum. Asian Americans attempt to formulate a new identity by integrating ethnic cultural values, Western influences, and minority group experiences. Alliances are made with other Asian Americans and oppressed minority groups. Table 5 shows the kinds of behaviors and reactions characteristic of each of the three types.

Table 5. Characteristics of Three Types of Asian Americans.

	Traditionalist	Marginal Person	Asian American
Self-worth defined by	Obedience to parents Behaviors that bring honor to the family	Ability to acculturate into White society	Ability to attain pride through defining a new identity
Behavior that arouses guilt	Failure to live up to parental values	Defiance of parental values	Defiance of parental values
Attribution of blame for one's lack of success	Self White society	Chinese values Minimal blame on White society	White society
Handling of prejudice and discrimination	Deferring and minimizing effects	Denying and minimizing effects	Anger and militancy

Source: Sue and Sue (1971).

The Sues intended their analysis to be descriptive rather than explanatory and to be used for heuristic purposes rather than for the description of actual individuals. They also reviewed research that suggested that Asian Americans experience significant emotional problems and need bilingual and bicultural therapeutic services.

Circulated widely and later reprinted in anthologies by the Asian American studies programs at the Los Angeles and Berkeley campuses of the University of California, the article by the Sues drew an angry response from Tong (1971), who accused them of "lunacy" and of holding "extremely dangerous views." Specifically, he charged that (1) their typological scheme was imprecise and lacked explanatory value; (2) the Sues had misinterpreted their own research findings and those of others;

(3) the article lacked novel suggestions for treatment; (4) the Sues' analysis, as well as analyses by other social scientists, was consistent with a WASP orientation and stereotypic in nature; and (5) findings that Chinese Americans are more conforming and passive than Caucasian Americans can be best explained by reference to historical events. Tong then hypothesized that the early Chinese immigrants to the United States were adventurous and not passive but that, in order to survive the racism perpetrated in this society, they adopted a meek-and-mild syndrome —a nonthreatening strategy—which eventually became a part of Chinese American personality.

Tong's attack on the Sues and other social scientists prompted a response from Abbott (1972), who questioned Tong's historical analysis of the situation of Chinese immigrants. On the basis of his own research in Taiwan and San Francisco, Abbott concluded (pp. 68-69) that the Sues' analysis had empirical support:

> The Sues have systematically collected data, analyzed them, and have presented their findings and their conclusions based upon these data—with considerable attention to methodological factors and their effect upon both the data and the meaning of their findings. Essentially, they deductively derive their theory from systematically collected data—clinical and empirical. Tong refers to numerous publications, [to] essays of his students, and apparently to one research project with a sample of thirty-four high school students and inductively constructs his theory free-hand, drawing extensively on secondary sources.
>
> While there is no implicitly superior value in either method of constructing theory, validity is considerably easier to safeguard in the method used by the Sues, who can always return to their data and their explicit methodology in the face of criticism or for further analysis. Tong, who has no specific data or explicit methodology, can only attempt to assert his theory with greater clarity and incisiveness. Any straightforward discussion of the inductive-deductive argument usually concludes that the two methods should complement each other. . . . Thus,

the Sues, using their deductive conclusions, can inductively advance hypotheses which in turn can be deductively validified.

Tong (1972a) charged that the research of Abbott and other scholars, using quantifiable categories of statistically significant findings, produced jibberish that could not represent the "sensibility" of Chinese Americans. Responses from Sue and Sue (1972) to Tong and Tong's (1972b) attack followed. In published letters, Elizabeth Lee Abbott (1973), a Chinese American coinvestigator on K. Abbott's project, criticized Tong, who, in turn, responded to her (Tong, 1973). Takagi (1973) joined Tong in attacking the writings of many social scientists as racist and ahistorical. A critique of both the Sues and Tong appeared, in which the interaction of historical and political experiences was stressed (Surh, 1974). Further clarifications of their positions were then made (see Sue, 1974; Tong, 1974). Finally, in reexamining the alleged success of Asian Americans, Suzuki (1977) concluded that some of the ideas of the Sues and of Tong were not valid.

In retrospect, the controversy served several purposes. First, it revealed the strong emotional feelings attached to the issue of Asian American personality. The replies and rejoinders were extremely heated; ad hominem assaults accompanied the substantive arguments. While such stinging assaults frequently obscure the content of issues, the effect was actually to kindle the ideas of those interested in Asian American personality. In personal letters to each other in 1980, Tong and S. Sue both agreed that the controversy, as painful as it was, served a valuable function in drawing attention to different perspectives and in stimulating others to discuss and to conduct research. Second, the individuals in the disputes raised as a fundamental issue the impact of racism. Some held that Asian Americans' experiences with prejudice and discrimination had strongly affected their personality. For others, especially Tong and Takagi, the theoretical and conceptual approaches of social scientists also reflected racism. For example, Takagi (1973) criticized noted social scientists such as Milton Gordon and Robert Park for their concept of assimilation, which, in his opinion, is based on racist assumptions. Third, the disagreements between the parties have in the main been over whether "sensibilities" of Asian Americans have been adequately portrayed. Chin (1982) has defined sensibilities as the outlooks, values, cognitive styles, behaviors, and personality patterns of individuals. Have research and theory adequately *described* and *explained* Asian American sensibilities? Finally, the direction of intervention has been a source of conflict. Some have advocated more effective treatment and therapy approaches; others have called for massive social and institutional changes.

Most of these controversies are not new to race relations or to psychology. Although some of the disputes were created by misunderstandings (as evidenced by various authors claiming that their positions had been misinterpreted by others), most represented genuine philosophical differences over theory, research, and intervention—differences not easily resolved through empirical research.

Personality Research

A review of the studies of Asian and Pacific American personality yields several conclusions:

1. The overwhelming majority of studies has been conducted on Chinese and Japanese Americans rather than other Asian or Pacific American groups.
2. A high proportion of the research has used student populations in Hawaii as subjects.
3. The typical design of the research is to administer a questionnaire to one or more Asian and Pacific American groups and to compare the responses with those of Caucasian Americans. Sex and generational differences are often correlated with responses to the questionnaires.
4. While nearly 100 empirical studies can be found, a few investigators account for a disproportionate number of studies.

Some of these characteristics of the available research

pose major generalizability problems. It is unclear, for example, whether the research findings (even though consistent) on Chinese and Japanese Americans have much generality for other Asian and Pacific American groups. Generality is also potentially hampered by the focus on student populations and by findings that Asian and Pacific Americans in Hawaii may be different from those residing on the mainland (Matsumoto, Meredith, and Masuda, 1970). Given these limitations, let us examine personality research findings and the explanations for the results.

The findings of investigations conducted over the past three decades can be readily summarized. Personality characteristics have been found to vary as a function of race and level of assimilation. Comparisons between certain Asian American groups and Caucasian Americans have yielded consistent results. On personality questionnaires, Japanese Americans have reported higher needs for order, abasement, nurturance, and deference and lower needs for heterosexuality, intraception, change, dominance, and leadership (Arkoff, 1959; Arkoff, Meredith, and Iwahara, 1962; Connor, 1974a, 1974b; Fenz and Arkoff, 1962; Meredith, 1966). Generally, the studies have supported the view that Japanese Americans are less aggressive, assertive, and individualistic than Caucasian Americans. Behavioral measures have tended to confirm findings obtained from self-report instruments. For example, Ayabe (1971) has found that Japanese Americans are more inhibited in verbal expression than Caucasian Americans. They are less responsive in the classroom (Hutchinson, Arkoff, and Weaver, 1966) and tend to be more accepting of bogus personality descriptions given by experimenters (Diamond and Bond, 1974).

Only a few empirical studies can be found on the personality patterns of other Asian and Pacific American groups. To some extent, Chinese Americans share personality traits attributed to Japanese Americans. In comparison to Caucasian Americans, they exhibit greater deference, abasement, and external locus of control and show less dominance, aggression, preference for ambiguity, and autonomy (Fenz and Arkoff, 1962; Hsieh, Shybut, and Lotsof, 1969; Meade, 1970; Sue and

Kirk, 1972) on self-report and behavioral measures. Studies have been conducted on the achievement motivation and needs of Pilipino Americans (Fenz and Arkoff, 1962; Kubany, Gallimore, and Buell, 1970), the resistance to temptation on the part of Samoan Americans (Grinder and McMichael, 1963), and the needs and deferral of gratification of Polynesian Hawaiian Americans (Fenz and Arkoff, 1962; Gallimore, Weiss, and Finney, 1974).

If Asian cultural values account for some of the personality traits found among Asian American groups, one would expect these characteristics to decrease with acculturation (cultural assimilation or the learning and adoption of the cultural patterns of the host group) and assimilation (the process of amalgamation or, in this case, the merging of the group into the host group). In several studies the number of generations in the United States has been used as a measure of assimilation.

In comparing first (Issei), second (Nisei), and third (Sansei) generations of Japanese Americans with Caucasian Americans, Connor (1974b) found that the number of the generation was directly related to the strength of self-reported "American" identity. Although Japanese Americans had higher scores than Caucasian Americans on a questionnaire dealing with family cohesiveness, Sansei were closer to the responses of Caucasian Americans than were earlier generations of Japanese Americans. Connor (1974a) also compared the personality patterns of Japanese Americans on the Edwards Personality Preference Schedule, administered to one group in 1952 and to another group in 1974. Hypothesizing that Japanese Americans have become more acculturated over time, Connor found that the 1974 group was more similar to Caucasian Americans in personality traits than was the 1952 group. Other studies have also confirmed the direct relationship between assimilation/acculturation and the loss of ethnic identity (Masuda, Matsumoto, and Meredith, 1970; Matsumoto, Meredith, and Masuda, 1970). Sue and Kirk (1973) discovered that, compared to Chinese American students, Japanese Americans were more similar in personality to other students at the University of California, Berkeley. They speculated that Japanese Americans are more assimilated than Chinese Americans are. Not enough research has been conducted on other Asian and Pacific American groups to allow for specific conclusions. As a general phenomenon, the more assimilated or acculturated Asian Americans are, the greater the similarity to Caucasian American personality characteristics.

To explain the observed personality differences between Asian and Caucasian Americans, social scientists have traditionally relied on culture. Abbott (1976) developed personality profiles for Chinese in Taiwan and Chinese Americans in San Francisco. Three similar components were extracted from the profiles of the two groups: (1) self-restraint as manifested by an apparent subordination of individual impulse to the group; (2) somatization of emotional problems; and (3) holistic perception in which the individual is considered as a part of the larger family. Abbott believes that these characteristics are encouraged by Chinese cultural values and socialization practices. The deference, abasement, low individualism, and discomfort in social interactions can be explained by the subordination of self to the family and group. Such an interpretation would be somewhat compatible with the perspective of Hsu (1971), whose theory of the Chinese family structure was discussed in Chapter Four. The traditional culture of various Asian groups has also been used to account for the personality pattern of the particular Asian American group.

The reliability and consistency of the findings cannot be denied. Nevertheless, some social scientists have recently taken issue with the cultural explanation for the findings and with the validity of the results. For example, Tong (1971, 1972a) has questioned whether differences between Chinese and Caucasian Americans can be attributed solely to the maintenance of traditional ethnic values among Chinese Americans. That is, the greater deference and compliance shown by Chinese Americans may be due, in part, to factors besides Chinese culture. Tong hypothesizes that in order to survive in a racist society, Chinese Americans may have had to respond in a deferential fashion. Suzuki (1977) argues that in order to explain the academic achievements of certain Asian American groups, investigators have erroneously applied the theory of "cultural determinism," whereby certain Asian cultural values encourage diligence, self-discipline, and achievement motivation. Indeed, Caudill and DeVos (1956) and Stevens (1975) have applied such an explanation in their suggestion that Japanese cultural values stress the kinds of behaviors that are compatible with White, middle-class ideals and that foster high achievement. Suzuki believes that Asian American attributes and mobility have been largely shaped by social and economic conditions in American society rather than by Asian cultural values. In his view, certain skills and traits are reinforced and encouraged in schools and in society. For Asian Americans, these skills and characteristics include obedience, conformity, punctuality, and respect for authority. Suzuki further speculates that the reinforcement shapes behavioral patterns that allow for employment in low-echelon white-collar positions. Data on income and education reveal that Chinese and Japanese Americans, despite having high educational attainments, still have average incomes that are lower than those of Caucasian Americans, once level of education is controlled. Perhaps, Suzuki concludes, certain cultural patterns, out of the array that Asian Americans may possess, are encouraged. These selectively encouraged traits prepare one for upward mobility but not for higher-echelon positions. The need for lower-echelon white-collar workers increased after World War II, and Asian Americans were shaped into these positions. In essence, Suzuki points to the broad context of sociohistorical forces and the social system as factors in the personality patterns and occupations of Asian Americans.

Advocates dissatisfied with the notion of cultural determinism have stressed the interaction of culture and histories in the adoption of adaptive strategies. This interaction approach is significantly more complex than that of the cultural determinism perspective. Whereas cultural determinism examines Asian and American cultural values and the extent to which individuals possess these values (that is, the degree of assimilation), the bicultural interaction approach includes cultural determinism along with other important considerations. How the social and political systems in the United States have influenced Asian Americans and how Asian Americans have responded are also examined. As an example, Sue and Kirk (1973) found that Chinese American students have tended to select vocations in the physical sciences and skilled technical fields. The cultural explanation views the selection of these fields as a function of Chinese cultural values that accord more respect to physical and biological sciences than, say, to the social sciences and humanities. Sue and Kirk, however, believe that the physical sciences and technical fields are often chosen because these professions probably require fewer interpersonal interactions, a belief shared by Wang (see Harris, 1981). The investigators also discovered that American-born Japanese are more similar in personality and interest patterns to Caucasian Americans than are American-born Chinese. The finding can be explained by the possibility that Japanese values are more similar than Chinese values to those of White Americans or that American-born Japanese tend to be from the third and fourth generations while American-born Chinese tend to be from the second and third generations. As mentioned earlier, Caudill and DeVos (1956) and Stevens (1975) have proposed that Japanese cultural values have much in common with American middle-class values. In contrast to these cultural explanations, Sue and Kirk believe that cultural determinism may be an inadequate explanation. Their suggestion is that the war between the United States and Japan may have forced Japanese Americans to demonstrate their loyalty to America and therefore to become more acculturated.

There is no question that cultural factors exert a powerful influence on the personality and behavior of Asian Americans. Nevertheless, culture may be an insufficient approach to conceptualizing Asian-Caucasian American differences or similarities.

At another level, personality research has created somewhat of a controversy over the extent to which the research findings reveal the true sensibilities of Asian and Pacific Americans. The controversy deals not so much with the reliability of the results as with their validity. Do Chinese and Japanese Americans possess as personality characteristics a greater tendency toward conformity, deference, and so on? In psychology there has been a long-standing debate on whether person vari-

ables (such as personality) or situational variables are more potent in influencing behavior. Tong (1971) has taken to task social scientists' interpretations of research findings on Asian
Americans. He suggests that the findings reflect situational responses rather than personality dispositions. Chinese Americans
may exhibit deference and passivity on some measures, but their
aggressiveness and adventurousness are demonstrated in other
areas (coming to a foreign country, gambling, and so on). In
Chapter Two we discussed Ayabe's (1971) study, which showed
that Japanese American students lowered their voices more in
the presence of a professor than in the presence of another student. The deference appears to be highly situational. It is clear
that the person-situation issue and the generality of findings
have not yet been resolved in the case of Asian Americans.

Another perplexing problem is that research findings and
theories or implications from the research may, in fact, mask
the true sensibilities of Asian and Pacific Americans. Let us take
the research findings concerning the male dominance over females. While there is no question that male superiority has traditionally been stressed in most Asian cultures, consistent results showing Asian American women as exceedingly compliant
and feminine do not reveal the subtleties or actual dynamics
that may exist. What is observed and what is happening may, in
fact, represent two different phenomena. Two examples illustrate the point. During a cocktail party with Japanese Americans, one woman asked her husband what time it was. After stat-
ing the time, the husband declared that they would have to
leave. The husband later confided to a few friends that when his
wife asks for the time, it is his cue that they should leave. Another colleague indicated that his wife tells him before leaving
home for a party what time they should depart. At the ap-
pointed time, he suggests that they should be going home. His
wife asks if they really have to leave. When he firmly indicates
that they must, she reluctantly acquiesces. The wives were obviously exerting forms of control that do not overtly usurp their
husbands' roles. These examples are not intended to suggest
that women are more dominant than men; rather, we are pointing to the discrepancy between appearance and reality. It is pre-

cisely these kinds of subtleties and dynamics that have yet to be adequately investigated.

Finally, the evaluation of the behaviors also needs closer examination. In our society, which encourages aggressiveness, competition, and directness, there is a tendency to derogate persons who exhibit passivity and meekness in interpersonal interactions. The value attached to such behaviors, however, is culturally determined. The maintenance of harmony, restraint of feelings and self-expression, modesty, and agreeableness are highly valued characteristics in other societies (Hirabayashi, 1975) and are not intrinsically undesirable.

Sex Roles

Early in the history of the Asian American movement, when concerns were expressed over racism and group identity, there was growing recognition of the plight of women as victims of both racial and sexual oppression. Angered by stereotypes of the docile and submissive woman, the exotic and sexy "Suzy Wong" type, or the efficient secretary or housekeeper, many Asian American women began to protest these stereotypes and to assume leadership roles ("Asian Women as Leaders," 1971).

Fujitomi and Wong (1973) have traced the historical status of women in China and Japan. Because of the patrilineal emphasis, the birth of a son was far more preferable than the birth of a daughter. A son could carry the family name (although the Japanese, for example, have adopted a practice called *yoshi,* in which a male adopts the female's surname upon marriage in order to maintain the female's family name). Women were discouraged from obtaining an education or developing career talents and were expected to be submissive, uncomplaining, and devoted to their husbands' parents and extended family. Although men often indulged in "promiscuous" behaviors (such as having concubines or additional wives), women were required to be pure and chaste. The traditional practice of "foot binding," in which the feet of Chinese women (primarily in the upper class) were bound so tightly that they could not grow, can be symbolically viewed as a means of fostering dependence, helplessness, and immobility. A number of other investigators (Fujiki, 1980; Hirano, 1980; Thein, 1980) have documented the problems and abuses encountered by Asian and Pacific American women.

The exploitation of women continued when women first came to the United States from China and Japan. Because of the exceedingly high proportion of male Chinese immigrants to the United States in the late 1800s, many Chinese women were forced into prostitution, after being lured to the United States or after being sold into slavery. Through "go-betweens" or matchmakers, Japanese women were frequently sent from Japan as spouses to Japanese men. Often called "picture brides," since pictures of prospective brides were given to the men, these women often had their expectations of prosperity in the United States shattered by the cruel reality of hard work, poverty, discrimination, and isolation from the familiar conditions of their previous environment. (It should be noted that the picture bride phenomenon relied on traditional matchmaking practices in Japan and was, therefore, somewhat more "civilized" than the tobacco bride period in colonial English America.) These historical events, coupled with experiences in the United States, have influenced sex roles among Asian Americans today.

Sex Role Conflicts. In general, research on sex roles and sex differences among Asian and Pacific Americans has not been extensive enough to permit strong or comprehensive conclusions. The available research suggests that women of Japanese ancestry in Japan, Hawaii, and Los Angeles are more egalitarian in their attitudes toward marriage than are their male counterparts, who are more male dominant in their attitudes. However, the males in Los Angeles are less likely to be dominant than those in Japan or Hawaii, perhaps reflecting an acculturation to the stronger equal-role attitude found in the United States (Kalish, Maloney, and Arkoff, 1966). Studies of masculine/feminine personality traits have shown that Caucasian American males rank first in masculinity; Chinese Americans, second; and Japanese Americans, third. Caucasian American females were least feminine and Japanese Americans most feminine in person-

ality (Meredith, 1969). Meredith and Meredith (1966), nevertheless, warn against the stereotype of Japanese American females (especially the Sansei) as retiring and compliant women.
Their research did not support this stereotype. They also found
that females tended to exhibit anxiety, whereas males showed
social introversion. Meredith and Meredith hypothesize that the
anxiety of Sansei females is caused by parental stress on academic achievement, dependency-independency conflicts, and
family and peer pressures over dating practices. Other investigators (Fong and Peskin, 1969; Sue and Kirk, 1975) believe that
conflicts between traditional Chinese roles and feminist orientations may exist for many Chinese American females. Sex role
conflicts also are likely to be present among Asian American
males. Although Asian American males may exhibit lower levels
of masculine behaviors, as defined in White American society,
their expectations of their roles as heads of household and that
of women as wives and mothers may, nonetheless, reflect strong
male-female role differentiations. The conflict they encounter is
over male roles in the United States and the changing behaviors
and attitudes of Asian American women.

Interracial Marriages. Personality patterns and sex roles
are strongly influenced by assimilation. According to Gordon
(1978), assimilation has seven basic subprocesses: cultural or
behavioral (that is, acculturation), structural, marital, identifica-
tional, attitude receptional (or the absence of prejudice), behavior receptional (the absence of discrimination), and, finally,
civic assimilative (or the absence of value and power conflict).
In this scheme, interracial marriage is considered an important
indicator and process of assimilation. It has often been used to
reveal attitudes toward race relations. Bogardus (1928) developed the Social Distance Scale to measure the degree to which
individuals would accept members of another group in certain
relationships. For example, accepting a member of another
group as a marital partner would indicate less social distance
than simply accepting the member as a co-worker. If Asian
Americans intermarry with Caucasian Americans, then implications for intergroup relationships can be drawn. Further, sex
differences in the rates of interracial marriage can provide in-

sights into intergroup and intragroup relationships. To the extent that one of the sexes tends to intermarry at a higher rate than the other, the implications for the psychological and social adjustment of those in the lower rate group may be profound.

In their studies of the rates of interracial marriage among Japanese Americans, Tinker (1973) and Kikumura and Kitano (1973) found these rates to be quite high; approximately half of the marriages in which one person was Japanese American did not involve a Japanese American spouse. Kikumura and Kitano also noted that the vast majority of outmarriages involved Japanese American women rather than men. Urban Associates (1974) found high rates of outmarriage among Japanese Americans and among other Asian American groups as well (see Table 6).

Table 6. Percentage of Outmarriages.

Group	Age			Total
	16-24	25-44	45 and Over	
Chinese				
Males	41	16	10	13
Females	28	13	7	12
Pilipinos				
Males	49	28	37	33
Females	50	28	12	28
Japanese				
Males	38	16	7	12
Females	46	43	16	33

Source: Urban Associates (1974); from data based on 1970 U.S. Census Bureau statistics.

Three facts are apparent. First, for Chinese, Japanese, and Pilipino Americans, the rates are higher among younger individuals. Presumably, the marriages among individuals from sixteen to twenty-four years old are more recent than among older persons, so that outmarriages have increased over time. Second, the rates among younger persons are high, ranging from 28 percent for Chinese American females to 50 percent for Pilipino American females. Third, sex differences in outmarriage exist. Chinese American males are more likely to outmarry than females, while the opposite is true for Japanese Americans. Table 7 reveals the

Table 7. Type of Outmarriage.

Group	Other Asian	White	Spanish-Speaking	Black	Other
			Origin of Spouse (in %)		
Chinese Husband	25	49	12	3	11
Pilipino Husband	12	42	30	3	12
Japanese Husband	14	65	8	1	12
Chinese Wife	18	59	8	3	13
Pilipino Wife	7	54	22	7	9
Japanese Wife	8	81	4	3	4

Source: Urban Associates (1974); from data based on 1970 U.S. Census Bureau statistics.

ethnicity of spouses for those Asian Americans marrying outside their groups. The vast majority of such marriages were to Caucasian Americans, and Asian American females were more likely to marry Caucasian Americans than were males.

A more recent study of Chinese American outmarriages in Los Angeles County for 1979 was conducted by Kitano and Yeung (in press). Their examination of 714 marriages yielded an outmarriage rate of 44 percent for Chinese American males and 56 percent for Chinese American females.

Why are the rates of outmarriage so high for Asian Americans? How can one explain the recent findings concerning the generally higher outmarriage rates among Asian American females than males? What can account for different rates among the various Asian American groups? In the absence of more theoretical and analytical contributions, it is not possible to provide more than speculative explanations for the descriptive findings.

Tinker (1973), Kikumura and Kitano (1973), and Kitano and Yeung (in press) have tried to explain the increasing rates of Asian American outmarriage. Some of their hypotheses are relevant specifically to Chinese or Japanese Americans; others probably have generality to other Asian and Pacific American groups. The possible reasons for interracial marriage can be divided into three major categories: Asian American acceptance of Caucasian Americans as marital partners, Caucasian American acceptance of Asian Americans as marital partners, and situational factors. With increasing acculturation and assimilation, Asian Americans tend to find Caucasian Americans more acceptable as dating and marital partners. Acculturation and assimilation may serve to reduce one's adherence to traditional ethnic values and to increase the internalization of White American values. Hence, the desirability of ingroup marriages declines, and the attractiveness of outgroup marriages increases. One third-generation woman remarked, "It would be impossible to even think of marrying a traditional [old-fashioned] Chinese male. He'd want me to stay home and raise a bunch of kids. If I had to marry a Chinese guy, he'd certainly have to have a much more open view of the meaning of a relationship" (Kitano and Yeung, in press). Indeed, rates of intermarriage are higher among succeeding generations of Asian Americans. With the increasing internalization of White American values, some Asian Americans may also develop standards of beauty emanating from Caucasian American conceptions of attractiveness. In describing her life in a Japanese American family in the 1940s, Houston (1980, p. 22) notes: "I found I was more physically attracted to Caucasian men. Although TV and film were not nearly as pervasive as they are now, we still had an abundance of movie magazines and movies from which to garner our idols for crushes and fantasy. For years I was madly in love with Lon McAllister and Alan Ladd. Bruce Lee and O. J. Simpson were absent from the idol-making media. . . . Although I was attracted to males who looked like someone in a Coca-Cola ad, I yearned for the expressions of their potency to be like that of Japanese men, like that of my father: unpredictable, dominant, and brilliant—yet sensitive and poetic. I wanted a blond Samurai." While one can hardly argue with an individual's personal preferences, and Houston's recollections point to a preference for Japanese *and* Caucasian ideal attributes, denial of ethnic minority culture sometimes results in racial self-hatred (Allport, 1954; Sue and Sue, 1971).

Morishima (1980) speculates that the evacuation led some Japanese Americans to encourage their children to marry Caucasians and to hope that their grandchildren would also marry Caucasians. This would, in their opinion, ensure that their grandchildren would be more "American" and that their great grandchildren would be truly "American." The reactions of those Japanese Americans apparently emanated from their feeling that they were evacuated because they weren't "American enough." Mizokawa and Morishima (1979) report that only four respondents out of 124 university students surveyed correctly listed the largest group of aliens residing in the state of Washington. When they were informed that the correct answer was "Canadians," the students responded that they did not think of Canadians as aliens while they did think of Asian Americans as aliens. Some Asian Americans may feel more "foreign" than Caucasian foreigners and desire complete assimilation.

Arkoff and Weaver (1966) found that Japanese American males expressed desires to be taller, heavier, and larger in the shoulders, chest, and biceps. Compared to Caucasian Americans, Japanese Americans were more dissatisfied with their height and the size of their biceps. Japanese and Caucasian American females wanted to weigh less and to be larger in the bust and smaller in the waist and hips. Japanese American females exceeded their counterparts in the desire to be taller. They expressed more dissatisfaction with their bodies than males and Caucasian American females.

The dissatisfaction many Asian Americans express about their bodies is apparently not a phenomenon of adolescence. Pang (1981) found that Japanese American fourth graders, male and female, had low physical self-concepts. Pang used a modified Piers-Harris to assess the self-concepts of Japanese and Caucasian American fourth graders. Nine additional items to assess physical self-concept were added to the Piers-Harris. Japanese American fourth graders were found to have significantly lower body images than White children of the same ages. Interestingly, Pang found that Japanese American children attending a Japanese American Methodist church had lower overall self-concepts than Japanese American children of the same age attending a Buddhist temple. She speculated that the models of power and influence in Christian scripture and tradition are

White, whereas the models presented in American Buddhism are Asian and Asian American.

Finally, for certain Asian and Pacific American groups in which a sizable proportion of members speak an Asian language, progressive assimilation is related to a loss of ethnic language. Assimilated members may not seek those whose primary language is not English.

Increasing rates of outmarriage can also be attributed to the greater acceptance in American society of Asian and Pacific American groups. As mentioned earlier, Caudill and DeVos (1956) have claimed that Japanese cultural values are significantly compatible with White, middle-class values. The achievement and professional attainments and "respectability" of Japanese Americans may make them desirable as marriage partners (Kikumura and Kitano, 1973; Tinker, 1973). Moreover, the stereotypes of Asian American groups are more "positive" now than in the past (Sue and Kitano, 1973). For these reasons, the social distance between Asian Americans and non–Asian Americans may have decreased. While it is unclear how skin color may also affect social distance, many Asian American groups are light skinned, which may make them less different from Caucasian Americans. The rate of interracial marriage for Asian Americans is many times higher than the 2 percent rate for Black Americans (Heer, 1974).

Situational factors have probably had a major impact on the choice of spouses. Asian Americans, particularly Chinese, Japanese, and Korean Americans, tend to live in urban areas. The consequence is that interracial contact is more likely to occur. Most Asian Americans do not live in segregated ethnic neighborhoods, again increasing the probability of interracial contact. In many cases, because of their relatively small numbers, Asian Americans may have far more opportunities to meet and date Caucasian Americans. One Chinese American male said: "I grew up in all all-white suburb. I was about the only Asian in high school so I dated white girls. I still continue to do so and I'll probably get married to one" (Kitano and Yeung, in press). Lastly, the antimiscegenation laws enacted in many states have largely been overturned. For example, the California prohibition of marriages between Caucasians and Asian, Black, and Native Americans was established by law in 1850 and was overturned in 1958.

Among two of the largest Asian and Pacific American groups, Chinese and Japanese Americans, the more recent data indicate an increasing trend for interracial outmarriages to occur predominantly among females. The most parsimonious explanation for the higher female rate is to assume that there are simply more Asian American females than males available for marriage. Thus, while the number of female outmarriages may exceed that of males, the ratio of outmarriage per total marriages for each sex may be similar. However, Kikumura and Kitano (1973) dispute this explanation. In their analysis, differences in the numbers of Asian American males and females cannot totally account for the much higher outmarriage rate among females. Instead, they propose several other factors for consideration. First, Asian American females seem to acculturate faster than their male counterparts (Arkoff, Meredith, and Iwahara, 1962; Meredith and Meredith, 1966). The precise reasons for this are unclear. In a racist society, ethnic minority males may be viewed as more of a threat than females. Thomas and Sillen (1972) imply as much in their reference to the historical fact that Black male–White female sexual encounters were violently opposed while White male–Black female encounters were not. Ethnic minority females may be better accepted by society and, therefore, allowed to acculturate or assimilate faster. As noted previously, acculturation is directly related to outmarriage. The "war bride" phenomenon beginning in the late 1940s, when some United States servicemen married Asian females, may also have hastened the feeling that Asian women are acceptable or desirable mates. Certainly, the large number of Asian war brides who were scattered around the United States increased the exposure of White-Asian marriages to the general American public.

Second, Asian American females may be more dissatisfied with the sex roles accorded to them in traditional Asian cultures (Fujitomi and Wong, 1973). Arkoff, Meredith, and Dong (1963) found that while Japanese American females and Caucasian American males and females were similar in their views of marital roles, Japanese American males expressed preference for male dominance in the marital relationship. With acculturation, females may find traditional roles unrewarding and seek out males who are more egalitarian in their conceptions of marriage. Moreover, with the advent of the feminist movement, Asian American females may have adopted even more egalitarian attitudes toward marriage, so that the distance between their egalitarian views and the views of Asian American males has increased in the past decade. Kikumura and Kitano (1973) speculate that females marrying out of their group are more likely than males to move up the social and economic ladder. More incentive is available for females to outmarry.

Third, certain factors—such as family pressures, the necessity to carry on the family name, "saving face," and physical height—may inhibit Asian American males from interracial marriages. Since in most traditional Asian cultures males are deemed superior and family name and ancestry are traced largely according to a patrilineal system, males may be discouraged from outmarrying. The family may view outmarriage as the ending of the "pure" family line, especially since children of interracial marriage usually marry members of the dominant society. Since females are expected to align with their husbands' families, they are in a sense "lost" anyway. Tinker (1973) has also proposed that Asian American males risk loss of face when attempting to date or marry Caucasian Americans. In this society, males are traditionally expected to take the initiative in courting. As mentioned in Chapter Two, *haji* among the Japanese Americans, *hiya* among the Pilipino Americans, *mentz* among the Chinese Americans, and *chaemyun* among the Korean Americans are important concepts involving shame or loss of face. By taking the initiative in dating Caucasian Americans, Asian American males are placed in a situation where they could be rejected by females and regarded as foolish by others and therefore experience shame. Another factor inhibiting male outmarriage is that Asian Americans tend to be shorter in stature than Caucasian Americans. In view of the usual practice for males to find a shorter spouse, Asian American males may be more limited than females in finding a suitable Caucasian American partner.

Fourth, the sex difference in outmarriage rates may be a function of the stereotypes in society. Asian American males are often portrayed as quiet, shy, passive, and socially inept. While they are also stereotyped as being high achieving and upwardly mobile, characterizations of their interpersonal behaviors have been largely negative. On the other hand, Asian American females possess more "positive" stereotypes, such as exotic, sexy, compliant, agreeable, and domestic. The masculine image of Asian American males has not, until recently, been portrayed, while the feminine image of Asian American females has been exaggerated. In a study of dating patterns, Weiss (1970) found that Chinese American females held negative stereotypes of Chinese American males, considering them "childish," "inadequate," "shallow," and "egocentric" in dating behaviors. Obviously, males may also hold derogatory stereotypes of Asian American females, regarding them as too short, flat chested, or fat legged (Tanaka, 1971). In any event, the more negative images of Asian American males as social partners may contribute to their lower rates of outmarriage.

Unfortunately, few data are available on the rates of outmarriage for other Asian and Pacific American groups. Such data could be used to test the feasibility of some of the hypotheses concerning the increase in outmarriages. For example, if Caucasian Americans find Chinese and Japanese Americans acceptable as marital partners because of their educational and economic status, one would expect less successful Asian and Pacific American groups to have lower interracial marriage rates. The only comparative study is from Hawaii, as indicated in Table 8. Outmarriage rates are high for all groups, especially for Polynesian Hawaiian and Korean Americans. Surprisingly, the rates for Japanese Americans are relatively low. Because of local cultures and customs and the opportunities for interracial contacts, the findings may not have much generality to the mainland.

We would be remiss in discussing interracial marriages if we did not discuss one of the inevitable outcomes of such marriages—children of mixed ancestry. Since the war bride phenomenon began in the late 1940s and since there were few

Table 8. Outmarriages in Hawaii for 1970.

Group	Number of Marriages	Male Outmarriage	Female Outmarriage
Caucasian	5,342	19%	17%
Hawaiian	105	73	90
Part Hawaiian	1,419	67	56
Chinese	334	64	67
Pilipino	1,013	45	46
Japanese	1,664	25	36
Korean	78	76	81
Samoan	131	46	43

Adapted from State of Hawaii (1972).

other interracial marriages involving Asian Americans at that time, most of the older children of interracial marriages are the offspring of Caucasian American servicemen and Asian females. More recently the war brides have been Asian females married to Caucasian and Black American males. Even though there are increasing numbers of "Eurasians," "Afroasians," and "Latinasians," surprisingly little research has been done on the children from interracial marriages. In his summary of a symposium on "Amerasians," Morishima (1980) indicated that the offspring of non-Asian/Asian marriages may have identity problems. Many are not accepted by the Asian American communities, because their mothers married non-Asian/Pacific Americans, or by the non-Asian American community. The major exception appears to be the children of Black/Asian marriages. In addition to potential identity problems, many of the children have been raised by their mothers after their parents obtained divorces.

Stereotypes and Trait Attributions

When asked to indicate what characterizes members of a particular group, one can usually enumerate several traits or personality attributes associated with that group. Such characterizations or generalizations may or may not be accurate. When the characterizations are not accurate—when they are false, based on illogical reasoning, or unsupported by data—they are stereotypes (Brigham, 1971). What are popular characterizations or stereotypes of various Asian and Pacific American groups? Unfortunately, little empirical research has been addressed to this question, especially for groups other than Chinese or Japanese Americans. Katz and Braly (1933) found that college students described Japanese as intelligent, industrious, progressive, shy, and quiet. Traits attributed to Chinese included superstitious, sly, conservative, tradition loving, and loyal to family ties. About two decades later, Gilbert (1951) replicated Katz and Braly's study. Although the uniformity of stereotypes and the students' willingness to characterize groups had decreased, many of the same traits were attributed to ethnic minority groups. More recent studies have indicated a "positive" view of Chinese and Japanese, who are described as intelligent, industrious, loyal to the family, quiet, and shy (Karlins, Coffman, and Walters, 1969; Maykovich, 1971; 1972, Ogawa, 1971).

As shown in Table 9, we asked several colleagues to indi-

Table 9. Trait Attributions.

Chinese:	quiet; family oriented; deferent; achievement oriented; thrifty; upwardly mobile; gamblers; Kung Fu experts; heavily represented in laundry, grocery, and restaurant work; males—passive, quiet, agreeable; females—exotic, sexy, domestic
Hawaiians:	happy-go-lucky; musical; naive; family oriented; lazy; obese; slow moving
Japanese:	quiet; sly; shrewd; initiative; industrious; ambitious; family oriented; well educated; upwardly mobile; assimilated; karate experts; heavily represented as gardners, professionals, and agricultural businessmen; males—passive, quiet, agreeable; females—exotic, sexy, domestic
Koreans:	assertive; hot tempered; hard drinkers; martial arts experts; outspoken; untrustworthy; male oriented; family oriented; upwardly mobile
Pilipinos:	gentle; violent and hot tempered; family oriented; sexual; males seek white females; males are macho; good dancers; flashy dressers; manual laborers; upwardly mobile
Samoans:	aggressive; easily provoked; family oriented; illiterate; related to one another; athletic; obese, slow moving; loud
Vietnamese:	family oriented; deferent; industrious; hard working; upwardly mobile, competitive; clannish

cate their beliefs concerning the traits attributed to various Asian and Pacific American groups. The task was not conducted in a rigorous manner. We simply wanted to gain some informal impressions of what the stereotypes might be. For Chinese and Japanese Americans, the characterizations made were highly similar to the ones obtained empirically from the studies previously mentioned. For the other Asian and Pacific American groups, there is no way to compare the list with empirical findings, since no studies of the stereotypes of these groups have been conducted. Interestingly, family orientation is a trait attributed to all these groups, and some characterizations appear to be inconsistent (for example, Pilipino Americans are described as gentle and violent). Some of the traits are positive while others are negative in terms of desirability.

Portrayals of Asian and Pacific Americans in the mass media have reinforced some of these characterizations: "With rare exceptions, Asians are always portrayed as waiters, laundrymen, cooks, villains, war-mongers, Geishas, house servants, gardners, karate experts, and prostitutes" (Paik, 1971, p. 30). The Charlie Chan, Fu Manchu, and Suzy Wong movies and television series such as *Kung Fu, The Courtship of Eddie's Father,* and *Hawaii Five-O* have exposed the general public to limited and, at times, quite stereotyped roles assumed by Asian and Pacific Americans (Quinsaat, 1977). Asian and Asian American stereotypes in the mass media have been the object of much protest, not only for being inaccurate, degrading, and limiting but also for practices used in the film industry. Many Asian American actors and actresses have been offered narrow and stereotypic roles, and central roles are frequently assigned to Caucasian Americans who are made to "look" Asian (Chu, 1977). Since many Americans have little contact with Asian and Pacific Americans, the impact of films, television, and print is likely to be profound. Certainly, mass media have made strides over time in diversifying the roles of Asian and Pacific Americans and have utilized them in leading and/or supporting roles—for example, in *Quincy* and *Star Trek*. Nevertheless, problems still exist, as reflected in the recent attempts to revive Charlie Chan movies.

Since certain trait attributions appear consistently in research and media presentations, Brigham (1971) has asked whether stereotypes have a kernel of truth. But how does one determine the accuracy of group characterizations—for example, the statement "Group A has characteristic X"? Such a statement may mean a number of different things. First, it can refer to a trait possessed by all members of a group. For instance, all members of Group A need oxygen to survive. In personality research, one rarely finds a trait possessed by all members of a group; moreover, if such a trait is found, it usually exists in all other groups as well, rendering the statement trivial as a personality description in cultural comparisons. Second, the statement may mean that X is present more times than absent in Group A members. This definition, however, is likely to be trivial as a personality description if X is also present in a majority of members of other groups. Third, the statement may be used to imply a comparison: Group A possesses characteristic X to a greater extent than Group B does. The problem is that characteristic X may be a low base-rate phenomenon for both groups (that is, the vast majority of members of Group A may not have X, but X occurs more frequently in Group A than in Group B).

Problems also occur when the statement is made within one context to individuals who are using another conceptual framework. For example, if one says "All members of Group A have X" or "X is present more times than absent in Group A," another person may point out that other groups also possess X. If one says that Chinese and Chinese Americans are family oriented, another person may say, "Yes, but so are Italians and Italian Americans." The statement "Group A shows more of X than Group B" often elicits the criticism that not all members of Group A show X.

A means must be found to avoid these problems and at the same time make a meaningful statement without claiming that all groups are identical (Campbell, 1967). One solution would be to specify what is meant by attributing a trait to a group and by indicating the importance of the attribution as a distinguishing feature. This would provide individuals with a common frame of reference in determining whether generalizations are false, illogical, or unsupported by data. Brigham (1971) suggests research on stereotypes which includes an assessment of the percentage of the ethnic group thought to have the traits listed, the saliency of the stereotype, and the certainty of the stereotype for the person holding it. Until there is agreement on the conceptual scheme being applied and until more sophisticated research approaches are used, it is fruitless to argue the validity of stereotypes.

The difficulties in determining the accuracy or inaccuracy of stereotypes are also complicated by the task of assessing what the stereotypes are and what ethnic group characteristics are. Presumably, one can show the validity of stereotypes if they are true representations of group traits. Sigall and Page (1971) have found that individuals may not disclose their actual beliefs and attitudes toward members of ethnic groups. Although persons may feel that Black Americans are lazy, Asian Americans are sly, and Jewish Americans are clannish, they may be reluctant to express their true feelings on questionnaires. Social desirability may inhibit their responses. Even if stereotypes are accurately measured, the ability to assess group characteristics is difficult. Our discussion of personality findings and their adequacy in capturing the sensibilities of Asian and Pacific Americans demonstrates the questions that have been raised.

Identity

The construct *Asian and Pacific Americans* was created for a variety of reasons: ethnic origins from Asia and the Pacific; general appearance; overlap in cultural values; common bicultural experiences; definitions given by federal guidelines; definitions by the Asian and Pacific American groups themselves; and similar responses and treatment by White Americans. One prominent rationale was the need to incorporate the group for political reasons: Asian and Pacific Americans formed alliances in order to represent a larger group; to advocate on behalf of newly emerging groups; and to achieve economic, social, and political gains that might not be achieved by each individual group.

The concept of Asian and Pacific Americans, however, is not universally accepted in the various Asian and Pacific American communities. With increased assimilation and acculturation, and with an increasing tendency for individuals to live in nonsegregated neighborhoods, many no longer identify with their own unique ethnic roots. On the other hand, such individuals—for example, a fourth-generation Japanese American who lives in a mixed neighborhood, speaks only English, and has learned very little about Japanese culture from her parents—may be treated as Asian/Pacific Americans by others. This tendency to be treated by others as an Asian may be exemplified by the following:

> One of our colleagues conveyed the following story to us. His daughter's fourth-grade teacher had just returned from a human relations workshop where she had been exposed to the necessity of incorporating "ethnicity" into her instructional planning. Since she had a Japanese American student in her class, she asked the child to be prepared to demonstrate to the class how the child danced at home. When the child danced in typical American fashion on the following Monday, the teacher interrupted and said, "No! No! I asked you to show the class the kinds of dances you dance at home." When the child indicated that she had done just that, the teacher said, "I wanted you to show the class how you people dance at the *Bon Odori*" (a Japanese festival celebrated in some Japanese American communities at which people perform Japanese folk dances).
>
> Obviously, the teacher was looking for a dance which would be different and which she could use to demonstrate that in a pluralistic society there are many forms of dance [Mizokawa and Morishima, 1979, p. 9].

The Asian/Pacific American alliance has had both positive and negative consequences. Political gains, sharing of experiences, and mutual support have resulted. In the process, however, some problems have occurred. One is that, among Asian and Pacific American groups, Chinese and Japanese Americans have received more attention and prominence, perhaps owing to their longer histories, relatively larger numbers, and stronger economic and political bases. Some groups have felt unable to play a central role in the alliance. Therefore, they feel that their needs and interests receive only secondary consideration. Another consequence is that differences among groups—distinct cultural values and bicultural experiences—are often overlooked when one tries to speak generally about Asian and Pacific Americans. Increasingly, groups have adopted the strategy of unifying when the strategy is warranted and then of attending to individual group needs when appropriate.

The issue of identity is also a personal one involving the question "Who am I?" The dilemma can be illustrated in Kim's (1980, p. 1) description of an incident with her son:

> Some years ago, my five-year-old son came home from school, shortly after entering kindergarten in a predominantly White neighborhood, and asked me: "What am I? Am I a Korean or an American?" Trying to be a good mother, I told him he was a *Korean-American*—he was born in the United States of Korean parents, and thus he had a rich heritage from two cultures. This did not comfort my son, nor did he seem to feel enlightened by the knowledge of his bicultural background. Instead, he protested, "If I am a Korean, why can't I speak Korean like you do? And if I'm an American, how come I don't look like the American kids in my class?" He paused for a moment and then delivered the final blow: "Besides, they call me Chinese!"
>
> He was not only bewildered and frustrated, but angry over his muddled identity as a Korean-American. The Korean and American parts of him seemed to be opposite poles, and a Korean-American identity that would somehow unite them seemed hopelessly elusive. It did not make sense to him that I was urging him to be proud of his bicultural heritage at the same time that he had clearly perceived that he was in some ways different from both his parents and his classmates.

Kim goes on to indicate that "What's lacking at present—in both the school and the home environment—is a conscious articulation of the decisions, choices, and compromises that must be made by the bicultural individual" (p. 101). She has accurately touched on the crux of the issue. Asian and Pacific Americans are exposed to the demands of two sets of often conflicting cultural values, encounter racism, and attempt to negotiate or build a bicultural identity. In a personal example, Sue (1980, pp. 8-9) has tried to illustrate biculturality:

> The "shut-off-the-fan" incident occurred in Honolulu last year. Dr. Francis Hsu, the past president of the American Anthropological Association, a Chinese friend of his, and I went out to lunch in a restaurant near the University of Hawaii. We entered the restaurant and sat down at a table. Above us was a huge rotating fan, which, despite the warm temperature in Hawaii, made us feel chilled. After a few minutes, Professor Hsu indicated that he was cold and asked me to reach up and shut off the fan, since the switch was above me. His friend immediately said that we should simply move to another table, since shutting off the fan might upset other patrons and the waitresses. Nevertheless, Professor Hsu insisted that the fan be stopped, and after some discussion, I reached up and turned the fan off. Later, we brought up the fan incident. I humorously mentioned that Professor Hsu's desire to shut off the fan represented an individualistic characteristic—that, despite the fact that the act might upset others, he wanted to satisfy his need. He has written in his scholarly works that rugged individualism is a characteristic of Americans and that harmony, situation centeredness, and kinship are Chinese cultural features. I wanted to point out that in some ways he is a rugged individualist and in other ways he is quite traditionally Chinese. I don't think Professor Hsu agreed with me, although he did say that I could publicly mention this episode as an example of biculturalness.

A colleague, Professor X, related another incident that demonstrates biculturality. As the director of an Asian American program, he had on several occasions interacted rather forcefully with deans and other academic administrators at his university. One day he told a colleague about some problems he had had with his parents. Instead of confronting his parents with his unhappiness, he stayed away from the traditional weekly extended-family dinners, claiming that urgent job-related activities kept him from attending. Professor X and his own nuclear family did not attend these dinners for five weeks. Finally, his father called and asked what the problem was. Professor X carefully and obliquely explained the problem to his father, and the problem was resolved. His colleague then reacted by saying, "That doesn't sound like you. I've been in meetings with you where you've shouted at deans and administrators. You've never been adverse to expressing your opinions." Professor X replied, "The dean isn't my father. I'd never even think of confronting my father or an Asian elder that way."

As implied by these incidents, the decisions and strategies used in bicultural adaptation need to be articulated. For example, what cultural elements, values, or behaviors are first to be extinguished through acculturation or assimilation? What aspects are maintained? As discussed in Chapter Four, Hsu (1971) posits that human beings behave according to rules and roles and according to an affective need for intimacy. In his scheme, acculturation and behavioral assimilation in roles are most likely to occur first. Asian immigrants, for instance, can learn relatively easily and quickly how to behave as teachers, students, or store clerks. Affective aspects such as kinship bonds are more enduring and are less likely to be extinguished because of exposure to White American society. What kinds of adaptive strategies are most effective as bicultural Americans? Is it possible to choose one's identity, or is identity shaped by environmental conditions? These are questions that have theoretical as well as applied significance and that have yet to be addressed.

Summary

In the psychological literature on Asian and Pacific Americans, one of the most controversial areas involves personality. In a series of heated exchanges, a number of social scientists debated the nature of Asian American personality. Unfortunately, the debates have not been resolved through research. Most research to date has examined personality differences between Asian and Caucasian Americans and has involved the use of personality inventories or self-report measures. The research has been criticized on methodological and conceptual grounds for its lack of validity and for its inability to reflect the true "sensibilities" of Asian and Pacific Americans.

Other important issues in personality concern sex roles, interracial marriage, stereotypes, and identity. Traditionally, many Asian cultures have been patrilineal and male dominant. Some individuals have voiced concern over the status of Asian and Pacific American women as members of an ethnic minority group and as females. Interestingly, the rates of interracial marriage are higher among Asian American females than males. It is speculated that Asian Americans and Caucasian Americans appear more accepting of interracial marriages and that certain situational factors have served to increase these marriages in general. To what extent are stereotypes of Asian and Pacific Americans valid? Many individuals have objected to the portrayal of Asian and Pacific Americans in the mass media. Research has found some consistency in the traits attributed to these groups. However, attempts to "confirm" stereotypes by comparing them with actual group characteristics are fraught with methodological and conceptual problems.

Finally, with respect to identity, the Asian and Pacific American designation is for the most part an artificial one. Between- and within-group differences exist. The most meaningful conceptualization is to view Asian and Pacific Americans as having a bicultural identity.

Asian Americans have often found it necessary to dramatize their social, economic, and mental health needs. Here a group of protesters is shown demonstrating against the proposed location of a stadium near Seattle's Chinatown.

The First National Conference on Asian American Mental Health, held in San Francisco in 1972, generated much heated discussion. Six hundred persons (twice as many as expected) crowded into the conference rooms.

Participants at the 1976 National Asian American Psychology Training Conference in Long Beach, California (funded by NIMH) examined how training could enhance the quality of mental health research on and services for Asian Americans.

Rosalynn Carter, Honorary Chair of the President's Commission on Mental Health, appears here with some of the Asian American participants at the White House reception given in honor of the Commission's Report to the President in 1979.

6

Improving
Intervention
and Treatment

Throughout their history in the United States, Asian and Pacific American groups have had various means of caring for the emotionally distressed. Chin (1982), for example, notes that for Chinese Americans counseling and therapeutic functions historically were handled by family and family associations. Later, church and missionary agencies played a prominent role in the provision of social services. Only recently have the mental health professions and the services of those professions assumed an important function for Asian and Pacific Americans, who became increasingly dissatisfied because of the inadequacy of mental health care and therefore adopted "political" strategies to foster policy changes.

Asian and Pacific Americans have suffered because of widespread beliefs that they exhibit few psychological problems. Even when problems involving immigrant status, delinquency, drug abuse, culture conflict, under- and unemployment, poverty, and family disruptions were prominent in the

128

1960s, they went largely unrecognized by the general public and by program planners and administrators of mental health programs (Wong, 1981). For example, in 1970 Elliot Richardson, secretary of the Department of Health, Education and Welfare, announced the establishment of a Center for Minority Mental Health Programs in the National Institute of Mental Health (NIMH). Charged with the responsibility of coordinating research, training, and service programs for ethnic minorities, the center gave primary consideration to Black, Latino, and American Indian groups. Ochberg and Brown (1973) noted several reasons for the initial lack of concern for Asian Americans. First, while the needs of other minority groups were apparent, NIMH was unsure of the problems facing Asian American communities. Second, Asian Americans did not have visible proponents who articulated Asian American interests to NIMH. Finally, the relative numbers of Asian Americans compared to Black and Latino Americans were considered small, so that attention was given primarily to these groups.

Of course, Asian Americans did have articulate leaders. The problem was to gain access to policy makers and administrators in order to make the needs known. In the early 1970s, it was apparent to those concerned with Asian American mental health that pressure tactics, political strategies, and educational efforts would have to be initiated in order to overcome misunderstandings about Asian American needs and to secure much-needed programs. In other words, the "squeaky wheel gets the oil," and if such tactics were necessary, Asian Americans were prepared to take them. (Note the potential conflict between the American truism above and the more traditional Asian truisms "the bamboo is strong because it bends with the wind" and "the nail that sticks out its head is the one that gets hit.")

Key Conferences

Several key conferences have played a significant role in defining the direction and tasks in the mental health movement.

San Francisco Conference. In 1971—as a result of contacts

among K. Patrick Okura, executive assistant to the director of NIMH, James Ralph, chief of the Center for Minority Mental Health Programs, and the Asian American Social Workers organization—NIMH agreed to fund the First National Conference on Asian American Mental Health. The 1972 conference, held in San Francisco, was intended to convene eighty-one delegates from throughout the nation to examine the mental health needs and priorities of Asian Americans. Conference organizers expected another 300-400 persons as participant-observers. However, more than 600 individuals attended, giving rise to much conflict and tension. Demands emerged for giving all participants votes as delegates, and tensions developed between different factions—for example, "grass-roots" constituency versus "agency-professional" groups, the "more militant" versus the "less militant," those "in charge" versus those "not in charge" of the conference, and "younger" versus "older" participants (Conference Report Committee, 1974). Underlying the tension were feelings of frustration and anger over the years of inadequate services and programs for Asian and Pacific American communities.

When Bertram S. Brown, then director of NIMH, appeared at the conference, anger was expressed over the lack of commitment from NIMH. Okura (personal communication, 1979) describes a particular incident:

> Following Dr. Brown's presentation about the need for the Pacific Asian group to form a coalition and get together and make their demands known to NIMH, he fielded a number of questions from the audience, and they became quite hostile, with a number of people taking the microphone and demanding and asking for a certain amount of money to be set aside for Asian Americans to use. Dr. Brown attempted to point out to the group that all grants were awarded on a competitive basis and if the Asians wanted their fair share, they should submit approvable grants. Following his presentation, Dr. Brown stated that he would not be able to stay for the entire conference because he had another commitment in Dallas, Texas, since the annual APA meeting was to take

place in Dallas. It was then that the group shouted they would not allow him to leave and if he were committed, he should stay for the entire Asian meeting. They even started to close some of the doors to the large meeting room so that he could not leave the room. During a break about thirty minutes after his presentation, we tried to quietly get him out of the hotel, but some of the group spotted the car that was waiting for him outside and were going to prevent Bert from getting into the car even if they had to bodily stop him. It was then that Frank Ochberg decided that he would get another car, and, in order for the group not to be able to see Bert, we asked him to get into the trunk. We were finally able to cart him away, since they did not see him in the car as it drove off from the hotel.

Bert continues to talk about his experience with the First Asian Mental Health Conference in a humorous vein, and when he refers to the incident he points out that this is what the director of NIMH must go through in order to earn his credentials.

Brown (1974, p. iii) himself notes: "Looking forward to one more quiet and ordered tête-à-tête with representatives of a newly organized constituency, I experienced instead a sudden immersion into the real problems of people in pain. . . . It was one which gave me a special dose of sensitization to what had been mostly an amorphous entity—the community. In retrospect, the sometimes stormy and quite volatile climate of the meetings seemed necessary to the process that resulted in the formulation of several major recommendations."

Both Brown and Okura felt that the conference alerted NIMH to Asian American needs, so that Asian American projects eventually were funded. Specifically, the Pacific Asian Coalition and the Pacific/Asian American Mental Health Research and Development Center received funding from NIMH. The conference also generated many recommendations—concerning, for example, the need to recognize the effects of institutional racism and the uniqueness of different Asian and Pacific American groups, the need for funding of effective programs, and the need for

Asian American research. Some of these recommendations are discussed later in this chapter.

Long Beach Conference. The first national conference held by Asian American psychologists occurred in 1976 in Long Beach, California. Funded by NIMH and sponsored by the Asian American Psychological Association, the conference was intended to address issues in the training of psychologists in Asian American research and professional practice. As at the San Francisco conference, tension was generated among the forty individuals who participated in the Long Beach conference (Dong and others, 1978)—tension in the form of conflicts among those who represented "community," academic, and professional-administrative interests. Some claimed that academic training was often irrelevant to the needs of Asian Americans and that the community should have control over research. Others felt that practitioners should become more involved in community research. Issues of control, power, trust among different factions, and the optimal mix of field and academic experiences were debated. Such issues are, of course, not new to Asian Americans or even to psychology, although the consistency of the conflicts points to the importance of the issues.

In the end, recommendations were made concerning more adequate training programs; increased collaboration among the community, researchers, and practitioners; better means of psychological assessment; and the creation of training centers. The last recommendation directly resulted in the establishment of the National Asian American Psychology Training Center in San Francisco. The center is now providing internship programs for predoctoral clinical-community psychology programs.

Seattle Conference. In 1977 the Task Force on Asian American Psychiatrists of the American Psychiatric Association obtained an NIMH grant to hold a conference concerning inadequacies in psychiatric training programs for Asian psychiatric trainees (Sata and Lin, 1977). These programs, conference members pointed out, frequently fail to deal with the adjustment problems of the large number of foreign medical graduates who come to the United States for psychiatric training. The programs also fail to offer culturally relevant curricula not just to foreign graduates but to all psychiatric trainees. And, finally, they fail to expose trainees to a culturally diverse range of clinical practica.

President's Commission on Mental Health. The 1977 meeting of the Asian/Pacific American Subpanel to the President's Commission on Mental Health was attended by twenty-five national leaders in the mental health field and supported by the ideas of many other Asian and Pacific American experts. At this meeting the subpanel sought to evaluate mental health needs, to critique research and service delivery programs, and to make recommendations for improving the mental health of Asian Americans. Many of the sixty-seven recommendations are consistent with the ideas expressed by others:

1. Mental health policies should acknowledge unique cultures, life-styles, and languages.
2. Asian and Pacific Americans should be represented in positions involving governance and decision making.
3. Bilingual/bicultural personnel should be available to Asian and Pacific American clients in the mental health system.
4. Training programs, service delivery systems, and research should be improved so that the welfare of Asian and Pacific Americans can be better promoted.
5. Racist practices must be eliminated.

Implications for Mental Health. In presenting these four conferences, we are not suggesting that other conferences have had little impact. Others can also be mentioned, such as the Dulles Conference of 1978 (which eventually led to the creation of the Board of Ethnic Minority Affairs in the American Psychological Association), the 1981 Research Methods Workshop for Pacific/Asian Minority Groups (headed by Peter Park), and the 1981 Conference on Innovative Mental Health Services for Asian Americans (organized by Angela Shen Ryan). Moreover, conferences on specific groups, such as women and the elderly, have been held. The four conferences discussed illustrate the activities within the social work, psychology, and psychiatry professions as well as the collaborative efforts among community leaders. One may also note the pivotal role played by NIMH in funding three of the four conferences.

Several conclusions may be drawn. First, major attention to the mental health of Asian and Pacific Americans is a relatively recent phenomenon (the first national conference was held in 1971). Second, national efforts to address Asian and Pacific American mental health needs are becoming more systematized. A network of leaders and organizers has been established, and the fruits of efforts are being seen in programs and policies. Third, although recommendations from later conferences tend to be more specific and concrete than those from earlier ones, certain themes recur at all the conferences. The appreciation of differences within the Asian and Pacific American populations—differences in histories, values, and perspectives—has been emphasized many times. Another recurrent theme concerns the conflicts among factions, such as researchers, those identified with the community, practitioners, and administrators. These conflicts arise from differences in goals and values, competition for funding and resources, allegiances to different constituencies, and misunderstandings. There is now an increasing call for cooperation and collaboration among these groups, since divisiveness weakens power and influence for Asian and Pacific Americans. Finally, Asian and Pacific Americans maintain that mental health programs, as a result of racism and cultural bias, have failed to accommodate their needs. It is this last issue that we will address in more detail.

Problems in Assessment, Process, and Outcome

Without adequately understanding the cultural backgrounds and experiences of Asian and Pacific American clients, therapists are likely to make errors in assessment, in the process of therapy, and in achieving positive outcomes. As an illustration of culture bias and its impact on understanding, D. W. Sue (1981) notes that even authorities on cross-cultural counseling are not immune to bias.

Several years ago, a group of mental health professionals were invited to a month-long program to discuss cross-cultural

counseling. Authorities on the subject came from many different countries, including Korea, the Philippines, Japan, Taiwan,
India, South Africa, and the United States. Each participant was
asked to present a paper on his area of expertise, and then a
discussant from the local Honolulu area would respond to the
paper. The first two papers generated lively discussion and debate. Soon afterward, however, several participants from Asian
countries refused to present their papers. They insisted that the
actual presentation of papers was unnecessary and that information could be conveyed through an informal exchange of ideas.
In an attempt to respect the wishes of the international authorities, the program director announced that the formal presentations would be optional. Nevertheless, he was disturbed by the
refusal. It was not until a few days later that the reason for the
reluctance was discovered. During casual conversations, a few of
the participants revealed their apprehensiveness over the format
in which their presentations might be criticized. They were not
used to the intense and direct criticism that often follows one's
presentation. The experience could be embarrassing and result
in much loss of face. Ironically, an international group with
interest and expertise in cultural influences had failed to see a
cultural bias, and one that had important effects, in the program itself.

Shon (1980a, pp. 726-727) believes that cultural bias
among mental health therapists can hinder an accurate assessment of the behaviors and attitudes of Asian and Pacific American (AAPA) clients:

> Traditionally, each of the family members has fair
> ly specific roles. . . . The American mental health profes
> sion often sees AAPA individuals from traditional families
> as pathological, based primarily on their own unconscious
> cultural bias of what is appropriate for mainstream, mid
> dle-class White Americans. AAPA children are frequent
> ly labeled as "dependent," family members as "overpro
> tective," and relationships between family members as
> "symbiotic." This is not to say that emotional disturb
> ances do not exist, for they certainly do, but the mental
> health system all too frequently compounds problems by

misinterpretation of both normal and abnormal behavior and interactions because of cultural ignorance.

Another area of cultural disparity that creates difficulty for AAPA people in contact with the American mental health system is the area of communication. American society tends to promote directness, openness, and honesty as its stated ideals. However, within the tradition of most AAPA cultures, communication is governed by many very complex variables. Among them are age, status, role, familiarity, concepts of obligation, shame and "loss of face," and many others. The area is so important and sensitive that the use of go-betweens is an important part of the tradition of many AAPA groups. Without knowledge of these important variables, many American mental health professionals make interpretations based upon their own cultural views and value systems around communication. Most psychotherapists rely primarily on direct verbal communication, and, therefore, this style of communication tends to be highly valued by mental health practitioners. Because of this, AAPA people are often seen as "quiet," "passive," "nonexpressive," and overall "resistant." In actuality there may be many messages being communicated, but not in the direct, verbal manner that American mental health professionals are used to. For example, AAPA parents have at times been seen as uncaring and unloving of their children because they have not been observed to express those feelings openly and verbally or through physical contact in front of therapists. These types of inappropriate interpretations by mental health people who are not knowledgeable about AAPA communication styles are further reflections of the insensitivity and cultural ignorance of the overall mental health system.

Shon points out that mental health professionals may misinterpret the meaning of family patterns and communication styles of clients from different cultural backgrounds. Obviously, other professions also exhibit this tendency. In discussing the implications of the frustration-aggression hypothesis (Dollard and others, 1939) for classroom management, Morishima and Mizokawa (1979, pp. 25-26) have indicated:

At the risk of major oversimplification of the [research] results: the higher the level of frustration, the higher the aggression. However, given the Asian/Pacific American cultural characteristics of reticence, nonassertiveness, and respect for authority, it is highly unlikely that such a relationship between frustration and aggression would exist for Asian/Pacific Americans. . . . For many Asian/Pacific Americans, frustration may increase without a concomitant increase in aggression until a threshold is reached. Once the threshold is crossed, there is an exponential increase in aggressive behavior—an explosion. . . .

As educators who also happen to be Asian/Pacific Americans, we find ourselves being consulted by teachers who discuss the asocial behavior of many of the Asian/Pacific American immigrant children. Careful questioning often leads to the following reported scenario: good behavior, better behavior, explosion. "Better behavior" is typically defined in terms of a decrease in the number of problems for the teacher. A quiet child who does not fight with other children is well behaved. A polite child is well behaved.

Our speculation is that as an Asian/Pacific American gets frustrated, the frustration tends to be channeled inward. As the internalized frustration increases, hostility develops. The hostility then gets expressed in a manner that is socially acceptable and understood in the Asian/Pacific American community. Unfortunately, the socially acceptable and appropriate mechanisms to express hostility and anger are often misinterpreted by the teacher. The misinterpretation and subsequent lack of corrective action by the teacher simply exacerbate the situation, and the internalized frustration and hostility increase until, ultimately, there is an explosion.

The key for the teacher . . . is to focus on behavioral change. It may be insufficient for the teacher to attend only to increases in socially undesirable behavior as indicators of potential trouble, since different cultures may express hostility differently. In the case of many Asian/Pacific American children, the teacher would be well advised to be concerned equally with increases in "good" behavior if there is reason to doubt that the student's frustration level has not been decreased. In short, in some Asian/Pacific American cultures an increase in politeness is the result of increased hostility and frustration. The aggression is expressed by subtle changes in behavior that are patently obvious in the community but which are, unfortunately, not cues for most teachers.

Another problem is that many Asian and Pacific American clients may fail to speak English or fail to speak it well. In an investigation of Chinese patients who were hospitalized in California state mental hospitals, Wang and Louie (1979) found that 38 percent spoke little English and 18 percent spoke no English at all. One woman patient was identified by hospital staff as Japanese when she was actually a Chinese who spoke little English.

Table 10 lists potential sources of discrepancy between

Table 10. Discrepancies Between Practice and Clients' Cultural Patterns.

Traditional Practice	Asian/Pacific Americans
Use of standard English	Use of nonstandard English or Asian language
Individual centered	Family centered
Verbal/emotional expressiveness	Restraint of feelings and self-disclosure
Communication exchange	One-way communication from therapist-authority figure to client
Silence a sign of blocking, resistance	Silence a sign of respect
Process of working through problems	Advice seeking
Ambiguity in therapy	Structure and concreteness sought
Distinction between physical and mental well being	Physical and mental well-being synonymous
Insight leading to change	Exercise of will power and discipline leading to change

Source: D. W. Sue (1981).

traditional values, assumptions, and practices in therapy and those of Asian and Pacific American clients.

Cultural factors are important to consider not only in assessment but also in the process and outcome phases of treatment. They can strongly influence whether the process and goals of therapy are appropriate or inappropriate. According to D. W. Sue (1981), one of four conditions is possible: (1) appropriate process, appropriate goals; (2) appropriate process, inappropriate goals; (3) inappropriate process, appropriate goals; and (4) inappropriate process, inappropriate goals. When processes or goals are inappropriate, the outcome of therapy is likely to be negative. For heuristic purposes, the case of a Japanese American college student is presented, and the appropriateness of therapy strategies is discussed.

> A Sansei (third generation), Roy K., experienced a great deal of suppressed anger over his parents' attempts to dictate what he should do and decided to see a therapist. Roy felt compelled to attend UCLA simply because of his parents' desire to have him stay near their home. His interest in majoring in journalism was also opposed by his parents, since they implied that a career in journalism would not amount to much. Even Roy's choices of friends and dating partners were deemed unacceptable. He was constantly compared to his brothers and to family friends who seemed to have the favor of his parents. Roy indicated that his parents, especially his father, did not engage in much conversation with him outside of criticism. He felt that it was nearly impossible to discuss matters with them. Conversations inevitably resulted in arguments and much sarcasm from his parents. Roy himself added to the conflict by using passive-aggressive tactics against his parents.
> Oftentimes, the strategy of process adopted by the therapist is incompatible with the cultural values or experiences of the client. We felt that Roy would probably feel uncomfortable and inhibited in working initially with an insight-oriented or feeling-oriented therapist. Asking questions of a highly personal nature, reflecting on feelings, or making depth interpretations could generate a great deal of discomfort and lead to premature termination of treatment. Our strategy was to use a more active, directive, problem-solving approach, to which Roy seemed to respond favorably.

Atkinson, Maruyama, and Matsui (1978) suggest that many Asian Americans prefer, and work more effectively with, therapists who provide structure, guidance, and direction. Ponce (1974) recommends that mental health workers working with Pilipino Americans should generally avoid approaches that emphasize communications, interpersonal feelings, feeling-touching maneuvers, or instrospection. At least in the beginning, an authoritative rather than an egalitarian therapist role is more consistent with the helper-helpee relationships that Pilipino Americans tend to seek. In a study of Chinese American inpatients and outpatients at a mental health facility in the Los Angeles Chinatown, Brown and associates (1973) found that the patients were not responsive to insight-oriented therapy. Instead, the use of medication, attention to practical problems, and the application of immediate measures to handle perceived problems proved most beneficial to patients.

Even when the process of therapy is appropriate, therapists may define the wrong goals, because of cultural bias. As noted in earlier chapters, mainstream American values stress independence and individualism, while traditional Japanese cultural values emphasize family dependence and role structures. Therapists may unwittingly exhibit their bias by defining clients' attainment of independence as a goal. In Roy's case, for example, a therapist might try to help Roy free himself from family influences in order to enhance Roy's functioning as a mature self-reliant adult. In some cases such a goal is appropriate. With Roy, however, it seemed preferable to move toward increased family cooperation that would allow him flexibility in making decisions without jeopardizing the family structure and without eliciting guilt or rebelliousness. Therapists who understand their biases and clients' cultural backgrounds are in a far better position to define appropriate goals.

Enhancing Match or Fit

Modes of treatment should provide a match or fit with clients' life-styles and cultural backgrounds. This was well recognized by Hobbs (1962), who in his classic article on sources of gain in psychotherapy indicated that persons have to maintain a "cognitive house" to protect themselves from the incomprehensibilities of existence as well as to provide some architecture for functioning. Certain cognitive houses or personal cosmologies fit with certain forms of therapy better than other forms. Those therapies that neglect the culture of Asian and Pacific American clients are likely to result in poor utilization of therapy, premature termination, poor outcomes, or little transfer of treatment effects. Admittedly, many problems or disorders exhibited by Asian and Pacific Americans are not unique to this group; and Asian cultural values and minority group status may be largely irrelevant in the problems of some persons. Nevertheless, if we have erred in our mental health approaches, it has been in the direction of ignoring the cultural backgrounds of clients.

As can be seen in the following list of a few of the clients we have seen, the problems described are not unique to Asian and Pacific Americans, although cultural factors and minority group status are implicated either in etiology or in the expression of symptoms:

1. A fifty-five-year-old China-born woman who worked in a garment factory complained of being physically beaten and intimidated by her husband. As an illegal immigrant, she was reluctant to complain to others and had attempted suicide on two occasions.
2. A fifty-two-year-old Chinese American man who exhibited paranoid schizophrenia believed that relatives, friends, and others were trying to kill him for speaking out in favor of the People's Republic of China.
3. A Japanese American adolescent was brought in by his parents because he was constantly using drugs, was arrested for shoplifting several times, and was associating with "the wrong crowd." He complained that his parents were too "Japanesee" and did not understand him.
4. A Korea-born woman married to a United States serviceman complained that she was unhappy. Her marriage had created negative reactions from both her parents and her

husband's parents. Because she was away from home, lacked English-language skills, and had no confidants, she felt lonesome and unable to deal with conflicts involving her husband.

5. A nine-year-old Chinese American student was referred for therapy by his teacher. The student was extremely shy and interacted with others only minimally. While able to relate with his parents, he exhibited a great deal of anxiety in the presence of others.

6. An eighteen-year-old Japanese American student was upset over her family's reaction to her Caucasian boyfriend. Her parents refused to meet him and on several occasions threatened to disown her. The reactions from her brothers was more extreme. They threatened to beat up that "white bastard." Furthermore, the parents were disturbed by her low grades. While she had done well in high school, her grades in college were now below average.

7. A thirty-five-year-old Japanese American woman who had immigrated to the United States when she was ten married a Korean American immigrant and was disowned by her parents. Although the eldest of her four children is now ten, her parents, who live within three miles of her, have never seen their grandchildren. Her husband's parents, who immigrated to the United States from Korea in 1979, have seen their grandchildren only in her absence. Despondent, the woman tried to commit suicide on one occasion and found herself watching while one of her children was drowning.

Better client-therapist relationships can be provided by (1) changing clients, (2) changing therapists, or (3) making appropriate therapeutic services more accessible. The first technique involves the pretherapy modification of the expectations and beliefs that clients have of the therapy process. Many Asian and Pacific American clients have little knowledge of psychotherapeutic services. They may believe that treatment is similar to that used in medicine, whereby patients are diagnosed, given medication or advice, and cured. By explaining what therapy involves, how resolution of problems can occur, and what client and therapist behaviors are usually elicited in therapy, therapists can help clients develop more accurate expectations and understanding of treatment. Many therapists wisely give pretherapy orientations as a routine matter.

The more difficult means of enhancing match is to change therapists or the therapy process to suit clients. It implies that therapists are knowledgeable about clients' cultural backgrounds and have skills to apply this knowledge according to their own therapeutic orientation and practice. Finding therapists with such knowledge and skills is difficult, since most mental health professionals lack training in ethnic minority group matters (Bernal and Padilla, in press).

The last strategy to provide more appropriate services involves the issue of accessibility. Bilingual or bicultural therapists may not be immediately accessible to Asian and Pacific American clients. Such therapists may be few in number or may offer services in locations far away from particular clients. In order to "match" clients with these therapists, the mental health system should have a well-developed referral process whereby Asian and Pacific American clients can be referred and have access to those therapists who have bilingual skills and/or bicultural expertise.

Major problems are encountered in the approaches involving changing clients and in making therapists accessible. With pretherapy orientations and explanations about the nature of psychotherapy, clients may develop a more accurate understanding of therapy but still feel that the approach is not likely to be beneficial. Individuals with cultural belief systems that are not well suited to traditional psychotherapy may still tend to see little value in talking about emotional problems. They may not continue treatment unless the therapy process can be made congruent with their cultural beliefs and life-styles. The strategy of referring clients to therapists with special expertise is limited by the small number of mental health professionals who are skilled with Asian and Pacific Americans. The approach of changing therapists or the therapy process to accommodate Asian and Pacific American clients may yield the best returns.

By developing skills to work with culturally dissimilar clients, each therapist can be a resource for these clients, and at the same time become more proficient in working with a wide range of individuals.

Therapist Changes. Three attributes are important in working with Asian and Pacific Americans: knowledge of culture and background, experience with these individuals, and the ability to apply one's knowledge and experience. We have already discussed potential discrepancies between therapists and clients in assessment, process, and goals of treatment. By acquiring knowledge of the culture and minority group experiences of Asian and Pacific Americans, therapists are in a better position to understand the verbal and nonverbal behavior of the clients and to seek forms of intervention that are consistent with the life-styles of these clients. Individuals who have had a great deal of contact with Asian and Pacific Americans are at an advantage, since they understand and are familiar with cultural nuances. In the absence of direct contact, knowledge can be acquired through didactic means. When students and mental health professionals are exposed to relevant literature, workshops, lectures, and courses on Asian and Pacific Americans, they become better informed of the values, attitudes, and behavioral patterns of this group. The incorporation of ethnic minority content into the curricula of training programs and into continuing education courses has been advocated by the American Psychological Association. In fact, the primary means of training mental health professionals in ethnic minority group matters have been through didactic opportunities. Nevertheless, these approaches to training therapists are probably insufficient as training tools because of the unclear relationship between cultural knowledge and skills development.

To illustrate that knowledge is necessary but not sufficient to become effective therapists, let us consider Chinese Americans. As indicated in Chapter Four, one major aspect of Chinese culture is the importance of family and kin. Whereas Western culture emphasizes rugged individualism and independence, Chinese culture tends to inculcate in its members values of solidarity, adherence to roles, conformance, and continuity within the kinship system. If clinicians know that the family is a prominent variable for Chinese, does this knowledge increase clinical skills? Conversely, suppose that persons familiar with mainstream American culture were asked by a foreign Chinese psychologist to explain how to conduct therapy with American clients. What would the response be? In comparison with Chinese, Americans are more individualistic, competitive, and verbally direct. How should knowledge of these characteristics be used in clinical practice? Social scientists discuss cultures and cultural patterns on an abstract level; therapists deal with clients on a very concrete level. The value of having knowledge of cultural differences between groups is that a context for understanding a client is provided. The potential problem is that the context is often confused with the person, so that therapists who possess some knowledge of Chinese culture may inappropriately use the knowledge in an almost literal manner. For example, one predoctoral clinical psychology trainee became very dominant and authoritarian in working with a Pilipino American student in therapy. His approach was based on his exposure to literature indicating that Pilipino Americans are accustomed to authority figures when receiving treatment. In this particular case, the approach was ill advised, since the student was quite assimilated and considered the trainee too directive. Ideally, knowledge of cultures must be developed along with experience in working with Asian and Pacific Americans. Only through contact can individual differences be appreciated. Only through contact can the therapist avoid confusing what is known about Asians and what is known about Asian *Americans.* Only through contact can the therapist appreciate the often confusing mixture of those things Asian, those things Asian American, and those things White American.

In summary, knowledge of the cultures and experiences of Asian and Pacific Americans is essential to increase the effectiveness of therapists. This knowledge needs to be translated into therapeutic skills and needs to be applied in a manner that considers individual differences. The best means of learning how to develop effective skills is to combine knowledge with experience.

In addition to knowledge and experience, therapists must devise innovative intervention strategies consistent with the client's culture and personal experience. D. W. Sue (1981) has suggested that since many Asian American clients experience a great deal of shame over treatment, therapists should change their technique so that they respond to clients' superficial complaints rather than to more depth-level dynamics. After rapport is developed, then the therapist can deal with those dynamics. The case of Mae, discussed in Chapter Four, demonstrates the application of an intervention plan not typically used in treatment. Mae was having difficulties living with her parents-in-law. In such a situation, many therapists would have tried to conduct family therapy, whereby family members could communicate and cooperatively move toward the resolution of problems. However, with this particular family and in view of the strong traditional Chinese values operating, family therapy probably would have failed. Some family members would have objected to the "outsider" (the therapist) and would have felt ashamed that the family conflict was exposed to another person. The strategy of choice was to have a respected third party (a relative) indirectly mediate the conflict.

In another case, Shon (1980b, pp. 18-19) was able to gain the cooperation of a family by using his knowledge and skills:

> F. was one of the first inpatient psychiatric patients I picked up as a medical student. He was a Filipino young man who had a diagnosis of schizophrenia, paranoid type. He had been on the unit about two weeks before I arrived and he was transferred to me.
>
> The previous therapists related that he had probably been psychotic for two or three years before his parents finally brought him in. He had been started on medication and was being seen in individual therapy and in family sessions. The previous therapists said that the family session had fallen apart and that there had been trouble with father. Father had not always given F. his medication correctly when he had gone home on passes and had also not always brought him back to the unit at the

proper time. In the family sessions he did not have much to say, and the therapists wondered how much he really cared about F., because of his behavior and the fact that he kept F. at home for two to three years before any treatment was sought. In trying to work around father, they had attempted to work with mother and older brother, who were quite verbal and expressive. Shortly after this, the family stopped coming to sessions.

In order to reconnect, I called the family and was able to arrange a family session in their home. Upon arrival I was offered tea and cookies as refreshment and, after politely refusing, allowed myself to be talked into it after mild urging, which is the proper etiquette. In the next twenty to thirty minutes, F. was not even mentioned. Instead, we went through the ritualistic small talk which was important in allowing them to find out about me and vice versa, without being too direct. I found that this was a very close, traditional Filipino family. The two oldest sons were married and lived within six blocks of the parents. They and their families, as well as the younger sister, were all at the family session. I discovered that father cared very much for F. I realized that he did not speak or understand English very well, but felt too ashamed to admit it. He already felt ashamed for having to bring his son in for help, which meant he had failed in some measure as a father. It was clear that he had gotten instructions by the previous therapists and was confused because of his poor English. When the therapists tried to work around him by giving instructions to mother, it was a severe insult and caused great "loss of face," so he pulled the family out of sessions.

Throughout the session I addressed all of my explanation, comments, and instructions first to father, even though I knew he did not understand everything and that others would have to translate later, but it preserved his primary status. Later we talked about delegating some responsibilities around F.'s meds [medications] and transportation to others, which finally occurred after father gave permission and okayed each assignment. At the end of the evening, the family expressed much gratitude that I had taken time to come to their home when

they knew I didn't have to. Father assured me that everything would be done to see that things went smoothly,
and from that time forward the family sessions and treatment plan proceeded without any difficulties.

Specific mental health programs to train individuals to
work with Asian and Pacific Americans have evolved. In San
Francisco and Los Angeles, NIMH has funded programs to train
social workers. Perhaps the most intensive specifically designed
program is the National Asian American Psychology Training
Center, which serves as a predoctoral, clinical-community psychology internship. It is located at the Richmond Area Multiservices, a community mental health center in San Francisco.
Interns are exposed to non-Asian as well as Asian/Pacific American clients and are able to rotate to the Chinatown Child Development Center, Asian Community Mental Health Services, and
San Francisco General Hospital. The internship is intended to
train clinical-community psychologists who have special expertise with Asian American populations. By exposing interns to
clients from these populations, by having a critical mass of
knowledgeable supervisors, and by offering unique didactic opportunities, the center has been extremely successful in training
Ph.D.-level psychologists who can contribute to Asian and Pacific Americans (Kim, 1981). One creative aspect of the center
is its use of a videotape library. The library has recorded the
ideas and research of practitioners, academicians, community
leaders, and administrators who have experience in working
with Asian and Pacific Americans. Topics on the videotapes include mental health, research strategies, treatment, community
dynamics, and culture. The videotapes are used to advance the
knowledge and skills of those interested in the mental health
field and are available to others from throughout the country.

System Changes. While changes in therapists can often facilitate more effective treatment with Asian and Pacific American clients, the system of mental health services can also be
modified. The organization and structure of mental health services—such as community mental health centers, hospitals, clinics, and precare and aftercare programs—affect the utilization of

services, the efficacy of treatment, and the overall well-being of communities. Findings that Asian/Pacific Americans were not well served in the mental health delivery system stimulated a drive for improvements in the system. Sue (1977b) has recommended three ways of providing more responsive services: (1) use of existing services, (2) development of parallel services, and (3) creation of new, nonparallel services. Let us examine the three and the kinds of programs that might be included under each.

One means of improving services is to make changes within existing agencies. Mental health facilities can provide training programs for mental health care providers and hire bilingual/bicultural personnel to serve as a bridge between Asian and Pacific Americans and the institution. By enlisting the aid of paraprofessionals, consultants, and ethnic specialists or by using team approaches whereby at least one member of the health care team is knowledgeable about Asian Americans, service delivery systems can be made more responsive. These procedures to improve existing services are the most widely used ones.

Another direction would be the establishment of independent but parallel services, especially in communities where Asian and Pacific Americans represent large numbers. Under this arrangement, separate (functioning relatively independently) but parallel (similar in function and structure to existing mainstream facilities) services would be created. For example, the Richmond Area Multiservices and the Northeast Community Mental Health Center in San Francisco, the Asian Community Mental Health Services in Oakland, the Asian Counseling and Referral Service in Seattle, the Asian/Pacific Counseling and Treatment Center in Los Angeles, and the South Cove Mental Health Center in Boston are a few of the programs that could be considered as separate but parallel arrangements. At San Francisco General Hospital, Lu (1981) has organized a psychiatric ward specifically for Asian American patients. In these programs, services are tailored for Asian and Pacific Americans rather than structured as a peripheral part of existing treatment packages. Experienced bilingual/bicultural therapists are used. For the most part, however, their main function is similar to all other mental health facilities; namely, to offer assessment and treatment to disturbed clients and to provide community consultation.

The third possible way of improving services is to create new, nonparallel services—new agencies, programs, treatment modalities, or institutions that do not have comparable counterparts in the mainstream mental health system. For example, a number of agencies have been created for specific groups, such as the Indochinese. Bilingual services, home visits, advocacy, housing, and resettlement functions are often provided. Many of these services are provided in multiservice centers. Mental health treatment still carries a strong stigma among Asian and Pacific Americans; however, when medical, social, legal, linguistic, and educational services are provided in a single setting, mental health can be considered an integral part of total care (Lee, 1980).

Community Intervention

Improvements in the training of therapists and in the professional mental health system represent one means of boosting resources for Asian and Pacific Americans. Another approach is to strengthen or build "natural" resources in the community. As indicated by the Asian/Pacific American Subpanel to the President's Commission on Mental Health (1978, Vol. 3, p. 782): "Asian and Pacific American people want a variety of choices when seeking mental health services. In this array of alternatives, it seems that most Asian and Pacific American people initially prefer to utilize indigenous community workers and natural community 'caretakers.' These caretakers may include ministers, relatives, prominent community members, and family physicians. Very often mental health care is provided via Asian and Pacific American primary care physicians and other health care professionals. In many cases, Asian and Pacific American people choose not to seek professional mental health care directly, except in the most extreme circumstances."

Natural resources, then, are those individual skills and strategies, interpersonal (for example, family and friends) support systems, and institutional systems (churches, herbalists, family doctors, folk healers, and so on) that are used in every-day life and in times of stress for coping. As Caplan (1972) points out, these resources are outside of the professional mental health sphere; that is, they are the usual and accustomed means, conditioned by history and culture, of dealing with problems. Professional mental health services provided by psychologists, psychiatrists, social workers, and psychiatric nurses, while not considered "unnatural" resources, represent a different system. There is widespread agreement over the importance of natural support systems in mental health (T. Kim, 1980). Murase (1980) notes that existing indigenous organizations (such as churches, family associations, hometown clubs, and credit associations) and community caretakers (for example, ministers, physicians, teachers, merchants, and elders) have provided care for distressed Asian and Pacific Americans.

The importance of support systems can be seen in the development of mental health services for Chinese Americans, as discussed by Chin (1982). In the late 1800s and early 1900s, family and various associations (of family members or of districts from which immigrants came) were largely responsible for community governance. The associations established rules such as how far apart restaurants or laundries must be from one another to guard against unfair competition. Interpersonal or organizational disputes would be heard by the associations, and counseling and legal functions were handled within clans and associations, not by outsiders to the community. In the mid-1900s, the associations were unable effectively to manage the complexities of the community. With increasing numbers of immigrants from different parts of China, they were overwhelmed by the magnitude of the problems. New services were needed. American-born Chinese Americans were not well integrated into the governance structure, and many new immigrants were not interested in joining the associations. Further divisions in the Chinese American community were evidenced in (1) the Chinese Americans who favored the Nationalist government and its Kuomintang Party and those who supported Chinese communism; and (2) Chinese Americans who were active in tongs, powerful secret societies, and those who avoided tong activities.

Even while the associations were still quite powerful in

shaping community dynamics, Christian churches began to offer assistance to the Chinese American communities. While church and missionary agencies attempted to evangelize the Chinese Americans, they actually functioned as social agencies. The teaching of English and the Bible, the liberation of oppressed women, the provision of havens for the poor, immigration assistance, socialization, and counseling were some of the functions of the missionaries. Although initially "foreign" to the community, church organizations gradually gained acceptance among many Chinese Americans and served to break down resistance to the utilization of resources outside the community.

The most recent development in the provision of social and mental health services is the rise of professional workers and young activists, who advocate political and social changes to help the poor and the powerless. Although many represent mental health professions such as social work and psychology, they regard themselves as more in touch with "the community" and grass-roots efforts than church workers are (Chin, 1982) and as more progressive than the Chinese American associations. In their view, the associations have merely maintained the status quo and the discrepancy between the "haves" and "have nots." The associations, in turn, criticize the young activists for their radical approaches and for their assumptions about what is needed in the community. Conflicts among the three community forces, while at times intense and disruptive, have set the stage for negotiations and cooperation. Associations, church organizations, and the young professionals have increasingly recognized the complex problems facing the Chinese American communities and the necessity to pool resources in order to deal with mental health and medical needs, housing, immigration, poverty, education, and language difficulties.

Community Empowerment. In a departure from professional mental health practices, Rappaport (1981) argues that empowerment of communities is needed. Whereas mental health practitioners have traditionally served as experts in providing services to people, an empowerment ideology is aimed at giving persons possibilities for control of their lives. Rappaport makes two assumptions. First, people and communities already have competencies and means of handling mental health problems. Poor functioning is a primary result of social structure and a lack of resources to develop existing competencies rather than a lack of mental health treatment services. Second, the most important task is to enhance people's ability to solve their own problems using their own means. It allows for a variety of locally rather than centrally (for example, by mental health experts) controlled solutions, and fosters a breakdown of the typical role relationship between professionals and community persons. Rappaport adopts the position that professionals often treat people as children in need of expert help and, in doing so, fail to correctly perceive community strengths and to effectively provide programs for assistance.

Rappaport's analysis seems particularly relevant to Asian and Pacific American communities. We have already indicated how aspects of the professional mental health system have failed to appreciate cultural differences or the life-styles and experiences of Asian/Pacific Americans, to form effective treatment strategies, and to utilize the existing social structures and resources of these individuals. While the importance of modifying professional services was emphasized earlier in this chapter, we feel that empowerment is vital in the strengthening of community resources.

For several reasons, empowerment has been advocated by many Asian and Pacific Americans. First, federal, state, and local funding sources have often neglected these populations. The lack of a strong political representation to influence funding priorities (Peralta, 1980), misunderstandings over the needs of Asian/Pacific Americans (Koseki, 1980), and greater familiarity with the problems of other ethnic groups have contributed to the neglect. Consequently, Pian (1980) and Lee (1980) have urged that Asian and Pacific Americans define their own needs and priorities and develop means to control resources.

Second, even when funding agencies attempted to assist Asian Americans, the programs that evolved have come under severe attack from various groups in the community for not responding to Asian and Pacific Americans. The rift between the programs and elements of the community is apparent in the criticisms. Administrators of the programs are frequently seen as outsiders if they have not established firm roots in the community; they are suspected of enhancing their careers by starting programs that give personal or professional recognition while exploiting the community. The research or service program thus developed is considered misguided because of the discrepancy between program goals and community needs; and the use of professional mental health personnel has often antagonized grass-roots elements (for example, those who strongly identify with the community and who actively fight for the alleviation of distress among the powerless segment of the community). As a result, Loo and Yu (1980) advocate that community forces have control over programs that are intended to serve the community.

Third, in view of the diversity among Asian and Pacific American groups as well as differences between communities, local control is a logical strategy. Communities are likely to have different needs, and residents and community leaders are in the best position to understand their needs and resources.

Community Networks. The concept of "networking" or linkage has emerged as a means of empowerment. Networking refers to the forming of ties and relationships so that the resources of those participating in the network can be brought to bear on the resolution of mental health problems. For example, community leaders, academicians and researchers, practitioners, administrators, folk healers, and consumers (within and between communities) may collaborate in the formation of mental health programs. Networking is neither new nor recent as a concept. It does, however, have special significance for Asian and Pacific Americans. Since various groups are included under the rubric of Asian and Pacific Americans, largely as a matter of convenience and expediency, and since within-group differences (for example, immigrants versus American born) are substantial, some means must be found to deal with this heterogeneity. When the contributions of many are pooled, the interests of subgroups can be conveyed. Collaboration helps to minimize misunderstandings that frequently occur between competing factions, such as researchers and practitioners. Improved opportunities for give and take also serve to increase feelings about participation and mutual influence. Finally, because of the recently emerging expertise on Asian and Pacific American mental health, the available manpower is still small. When collaborative linkages are formed, the chances to utilize the available expertise are greatly improved.

Summary

The mental health movement among Asian and Pacific Americans is relatively young. Frustrated by unmet social and psychological needs, Asian and Pacific Americans have struggled to gain recognition that problems, indeed, exist and that services have failed to respond effectively to these needs. Mental health conferences were helpful in demonstrating the tasks that are critical to address. Bilingual/bicultural therapeutic approaches, systems changes, and community empowerment are some of the important directions for future efforts. Table 11 shows the levels of intervention.

Table 11. Levels of Intervention.

Level	Therapy	Professional Systems	Community
Purpose:	Enhance assessment, process, and outcomes	Increase utilization and responsiveness	Increase self-help
Principle:	Match or fit	Match or fit	Use existing resources with technical assistance
Means:	(1) Change clients through pretherapy interventions	(1) Change existing agencies	(1) Empowerment
	(2) Provide appropriate therapists	(2) Develop independent but parallel services	(2) Networking and collaboration
	(a) Know culture and minority group status	(3) Create new, nonparallel services	
	(b) Gain experience and appreciate individual differences		
	(c) Translate skills in practice and use innovative strategies		
	(3) Give clients access to bilingual and appropriate therapists		

7

Advancing Research and Theory for Improved Care

Research refers to systematic inquiry of a theoretical or data-gathering nature with the aim of solving problems (Miyamoto, 1980). These problems include *prediction* (finding variables or a set of variables that correlate in a high and consistent manner with another variable of interest), *understanding* (discovering cause-effect relationships), and *control* (finding interventions that can achieve a desired outcome). Through observations, correlational techniques, or experimental designs in the field or in a laboratory, data can be collected and theories can be formulated and tested. In this chapter, issues on research with Asian and Pacific Americans are examined. These issues include (1) the controversy over the value of research for ethnic minority groups in general and Asian and Pacific Americans in particular, (2) the current state of research, and (3) research priorities for the future.

157

Value of Research

Investigators have bemoaned the quality and quantity of research on ethnic minority groups (Sue, Ito, and Bradshaw, 1982). At the same time, the value of "abstract" and "theoretical" research has been questioned. In view of the multitude of problems facing ethnic minority communities, some critics have demanded more "relevant" and "applied" research that can help solve social ills (Liu, 1980). Often, however, the resolution of social problems has been aided by theory and theory testing, and much applied research has failed to generate meaningful and practical applications. Therefore, simply changing our aim from theoretical to applied research may not increase actual application.

Other critics object to any kind of research because they seriously believe that it cannot solve problems. Social scientists investigating certain issues often come to different and conflicting conclusions. What are the effects of busing? Do ethnic minority group individuals have a positive or negative self-identity? Are there kernels of truth to stereotypes? Are there racial differences in intelligence that are genetically determined? One can find empirical research supporting either side. This is also true of the physical or biological sciences. The effects of saccharine in low-calorie diets, of DMSO as a healing agent, and of the defoliant Agent Orange are still debated in the scientific literature. As a result, the public has become increasingly skeptical of research findings in providing answers to problems. Many minority group persons, seeing the need for social changes, view research as an academic exercise and advocate social and political action rather than theory building or data collection. In advocating the attainment of power, however, they often overlook a critical element. To be effective in promoting human welfare, power must be coupled with knowledge. What do we change to? How effective are new programs and policies? These questions are generally best answered through research.

A single study or piece of research rarely influences social policy or action to any profound degree. If research "works," it does so as a result of systematic efforts over time. McGrath

(1980) examined the relationship between social science and social action, as revealed in the *Journal of Social Issues* for the past thirty-six years. Initially, the themes reflected a recognition of the urgency of world problems and a boundless optimism over the ability of social science to apply its findings to problems. Then doubts arose over the efficacy of social science methods when applied. Finally, in the 1970s, McGrath saw a period of bitter disillusionment about social science—not because research cannot affect social policy but, rather, because social action research can be used for evil as well as good. These fears, of course, are not new in psychology and are not restricted to research dealing with ethnic minorities. For example, in their debate over Walden Two, B. F. Skinner and Carl Rogers raised the issue over the prospect of human engineering. Skinner's point was that since control over human behavior is within the realm of reality, we must ensure that those who utilize behavioral techniques will do so for the betterment of mankind and not for personal aggrandizement (see, for example, Rogers and Skinner, 1956; Skinner, 1971).

McGrath's analysis also brings out another source of criticism of research: that findings can be used to the detriment of minority groups. In the foreword to *Racism and Psychiatry* (Thomas and Sillen, 1972), Kenneth Clark, past president of the American Psychological Association, indicates that social science research often reflects the trends of society: "Probably the most disturbing insight obtained from the relentless clarity with which this book documents the case of racism in American psychiatry is the ironic fact that the students, research workers, and professionals in the behavioral sciences—like members of the clergy and educators—are no more immune by virtue of their values and training to the disease and superstition of American racism than is the average man" (p. xii). For whom the research is done and for what purpose are the two key issues that must be addressed, according to Hirata (1980). She questions whether research is value free; researchers cannot simply assume that their work is conducted on behalf of ethnic minority groups and will yield results that promote the welfare of these groups.

Another related issue has to do with the control of research. Because of the potential for detrimental consequences of investigations, many Asian and Pacific Americans have advocated that researchers relinquish some of their control over research activities. Park (1980) proposes that community or ethnic minority research include the participation of those who are being studied. The Asian/Pacific American Subpanel to the President's Commission on Mental Health (1978) made a similar appeal, calling for research that is sanctioned by the community and that represents a collaborative effort between researchers and community persons. Some researchers, however, are reluctant to share the control and direction of research, especially with members of the group or community being studied. They fear that community groups may exert censorship over the findings, may not understand necessary research strategies and methods, and may force the adoption of poor research methods. From the perspective of community groups, especially ethnic minorities, researchers are often, at best, outsiders whose research will not benefit the community or, at worst, outsiders whose work will be detrimental to ethnic minority groups by perpetuating stereotypes or by an emphasis on personality, behavioral, or cultural deficits of these groups.

There is increasing recognition that collaboration between researchers and community participants is necessary (Montero, 1977). Researchers need the sanctioning and input of community leaders, community institutions, and the subjects themselves in order to gain access to the ethnic community and to construct data collection procedures that yield reliable and valid findings. Ethnic minority communities are in need of the technical expertise and resources that researchers frequently have. Community research should be a joint venture in which researchers and the community define the research problem and the benefit to the participating community is tangible (Park, 1980).

Current State of Research

Two recent annotated bibliographies (Doi, Lin, and Vohra-Sahu, 1981; Morishima and others, 1979) identified 400-

550 items loosely relevant to Asian and Pacific American mental health. The research to date has the following characteristics:

1. The research typically measures attitudes, traits, or behaviors—as evidenced in studies of the utilization of mental health facilities, attitudes toward mental health and treatment, self-reports of childrearing practices, generational differences in assimilation, the assessment of needs, and personality characteristics. Some studies employ measures—for instance, the Minnesota Multiphasic Personality Inventory—that are widely used and standardized on Caucasian Americans; others use questionnaires or measures specifically devised for Asian and Pacific Americans. Whether or not the measures take into account language (for example, providing subjects with questionnaires in English and in an Asian language), potential problems exist. Instruments standardized on Caucasian Americans may reflect culture bias and response sets that affect the validity of the instruments (Dohrenwend and Dohrenwend, 1969) for Asian and Pacific Americans. Questionnaires devised for Asian and Pacific American groups may appear to have face validity, but their concurrent or predictive validity is uncertain.

2. Caucasian Americans are often used as a comparison group. Such comparisons allow one to discover similarities and differences between groups and to gain insight into etic (universal) characteristics and emic (culture-specific) characteristics. Nevertheless, several investigators have recently criticized the comparative approach to research. Olmedo (1979) suggests that the approach downplays the study of individual differences within an ethnic minority group and unintentionally sets as standards for behavior the norms derived from the dominant (Caucasian American) group in our society. Korchin's (1980) experience is illustrative. He was collaborating with a colleague on research involving competency and achievement among Black Americans. A paper from their work, submitted for publication, was rejected because one reviewer felt the study should have included a White control group. Why should the study include a White control group when the primary interest was in Black Americans? Are studies of White Americans required to include Black control groups? The issues raised by Korchin are

meaningful. They suggest that the comparative approach, however useful, should not devalue the study of ethnic minority groups per se.

3. Most research on Asian and Pacific Americans has involved unsophisticated research designs and is descriptive rather than explanatory. Past empirical studies have been primarily correlational and confined to narrow populations (such as university students or mental health clients). For example, many of the studies of Japanese American personality by Arkoff and his colleagues (cited in Chapter Five) have simply involved the administration of the Edwards Personal Preference Schedule to Japanese and Caucasian American students. Differences between the two groups are interpreted as reflecting the socialization practices in Japanese and American cultures. Such descriptive and observational data are of course needed; and, as indicated by Miyamoto (1980), highly sophisticated research designs may be inappropriate in an area where the knowledge base is limited. Nevertheless, Asian and Pacific American research can be greatly enhanced with more experimental and multivariate research designs that go beyond descriptions and that include nonstudent as well as student populations. Hirata (1980) has also suggested that research should be addressed not merely to "symptoms" but also to the causes of the symptoms. She feels that researchers are often reluctant to examine the roots of problems, since it requires that they make explicit their values, which may or may not agree with those of the persons being studied.

4. Relatively little research has been devoted to theory testing. For example, as indicated in Chapter Four, critical tests for the adequacy of the theoretical formulations of Hsu and DeVos on family patterns are virtually absent. It is not clear why this is the case, although several factors are important to consider. First, social scientists have been far more interested in studying Black Americans than Asian and Pacific Americans. Second, Asian and Pacific Americans constitute only about 2 percent of the population of the United States. Problems in obtaining funds for research, in finding adequate samples to study, and in devising research that takes into account bilingual and bi-

cultural factors (and the possible attendant costs) may discourage more investigations on this population. Third, theory building and theory testing often require an adequate knowledge base. In the absence of a broad knowledge base, social scientists are more likely to emphasize descriptive studies.

5. Because of the strong interest in cross-cultural comparisons, within-culture analysis for Asian and Pacific Americans has not been extensively made. The single exception is in the area of assimilation. Assimilation is measured by self-identity (the extent to which individuals consider themselves to be "American" versus "Chinese," "Japanese," "Pilipino," and so on); the number of generations in the United States; ability to speak an Asian or Pacific Island language; the proportion of own ethnic friends versus Caucasian friends; social distance from Caucasian Americans; or attitudes, values, or behaviors that are similar to those of Caucasian Americans. The degree of assimilation is then correlated with personality attributes or other behaviors and attitudes. In previous chapters, especially in Chapter Five, we indicated that assimilation is a significant predictor of personality characteristics such as dominance and compliance, alcohol consumption, adoption of sex role patterns, and attitudes toward childrearing. Investigators often have attempted to find the relationship between various indices of assimilation—for example, between place of birth (foreign or American born) and self-identity or between the ability to speak an ethnic language and the ethnicity of one's friends.

The level of assimilation and acculturation undoubtedly accounts for a significant proportion of the variance in the attitudes and behaviors of many Asian and Pacific Americans. Other important questions, however, must be addressed. One involves the process of assimilation: Does it proceed uniformly, or are some attitudes and behaviors more resistant to assimilation than others? Sue, Zane, and Ito (1979) have found that different measures of assimilation may not be significantly related to each other. They used three assimilation measures—number of generations in the United States, ability to speak the ethnic language, and proportion of Caucasian versus Asian friends—and obtained moderately high correlations between Generation-

Speaking and Speaking-Friends; the correlation of Generation-Friends, however, was insignificant.

A second question deals with why some ethnic values or behaviors appear to extinguish faster than others. Hsu (1971) has suggested that Chinese Americans find it relatively easy to learn role and rule relationships—for example, the rules of conduct in playing occupational or social roles in the United States. What seems difficult to change or to extinguish are ethnic behaviors and values that involve affective and intimate relationships learned in the family. For instance, strong affections (whether positive or negative) toward one's family and situation centeredness (as opposed to individualism) may be the most resistant to change during progressive assimilation. The field of Asian American research is in need of more investigations into the differential impact of assimilation.

A final question involves the meaning of biculturality. Assimilation measures are usually unidimensional, since they place individuals on a continuum ranging from "ethnic" to "American." Measures of this kind fail to capture the interaction effects of both cultures in creating attitudes or behaviors that cannot be predicted from a knowledge of each culture. Banks and associates (1977) found that Black Americans who received negative evaluations from other Blacks on their performance of certain tasks exhibited lower self-esteem but that their self-esteem was unchanged when they received derogatory evaluations from Whites. Banks and his colleagues argue that Blacks have developed functional strategies to deal with a hostile racial environment. Evaluations from Whites are seen as biased and racially motivated. It is highly likely that Asian and Pacific Americans have devised strategies to deal with their social environment in the United States—strategies that cannot be predicted by knowledge of ethnic and American cultures.

6. Nearly all the research on Asian and Pacific Americans has been conducted on Chinese and Japanese Americans, perhaps because of their longer histories in the United States, their larger numbers, or both. The 1980 U.S. Census indicates, however, that major shifts in population have occurred. Whereas Japanese Americans were the largest group a decade ago, the ranking according to size of groups is now Chinese, Pilipino,

Japanese, and Korean Americans, in descending order. The changes in the numbers of Asian and Pacific Americans result primarily from changes in United States immigration policy. Proportionately, some groups have increased geometrically in size. For example, in 1970 the number of Korean Americans was estimated to be approximately 80,000. In 1980 the count was 355,000—a 400 percent increase. The number of Indochinese Americans was so small in 1970 that no estimate was made. In 1980 Indochinese Americans numbered 270,000—a tremendous increase. Given the larger numbers of specific groups among the Asian and Pacific Americans, there may well be changes in the quantity of research conducted on them.

7. Most of the empirical research on Asian and Pacific Americans has been conducted by Caucasian Americans. Ideally, the race or ethnicity of the researcher should have no bearing on the quality of the work. In practice, however, there is considerable controversy over the ethnic similarity or dissimilarity of the researcher and the group being studied. Some persons believe that only members of a particular group should conduct research on that group. For example, only individuals of Chinese descent should conduct research on Chinese Americans. Those who take this position contend that Caucasian Americans should not conduct research on Chinese Americans; those who take an extreme position contend also that Japanese Americans should not conduct research on Chinese Americans. The ethnicity of the researcher, then, would be an important factor to consider.

Others feel that qualifications and ethnic sensitivity, and not ethnicity, should govern the issue about who should conduct the research. Brazziel (1973, p. 41) suggests that qualifications and sensitivity are related to ethnicity: "Today's White researchers are perhaps counterproductive in Black communities, not because they are White but because they are poorly trained." Arguing that White researchers have less credibility than Black researchers in Black communities and that they are often affected by their own training, which may not have covered the problems of racism, Brazziel concludes that research in Black communities should be conducted by Blacks.

We believe that limiting ethnic research to researchers who

are ethnically similar to the group being studied is unwise and impractical. The manpower shortage of Asian and Pacific American researchers is an obvious pragmatic consideration. Ultimately, the qualifications, sensitivity, and credibility of the researchers should dictate who does research on what populations. Furthermore, race relations, racism, and culture are issues that must be addressed by all Americans. The fact that some nonethnic researchers have conducted poor or culturally biased research cannot negate the valuable contributions made by other such researchers. In view of the lack of more Asian and Pacific American social scientists and the special insights and sensitivities that frequently come from ethnic perspectives, there should be a special effort to train and recruit ethnic group researchers and to elicit the input and assistance of insiders.

8. Much of the literature on Asian and Pacific American mental health is repetitious, multidisciplinary, and nonempirical. Particularly during the 1970s, recurrent themes can be seen in the literature. These themes, which persist in the literature today, involve critiques of the model minority status or the success of Asian and Pacific Americans in society; the impact of racism; the mental health problems encountered; and the inadequacies of mental health services. The themes are repeated because the writers probably have been intent on dispelling the persistent assumption that Asian and Pacific Americans are extraordinarily well adjusted or possess unusually strong resources. That is, the writers have sought to demonstrate problems in the groups without implying that those problems exist simply because of deviations from mainstream White American norms in behavior or attitudes.

Since minority group status and culture are relevant topics for many disciplines, those outside the mental health field have contributed to the literature. Historians, economists, political scientists, and others have also examined the status of Asian and Pacific Americans. They undoubtedly have offered insights, ideas, and perspectives not traditionally articulated by psychologists, psychiatrists, social workers, sociologists, or psychological anthropologists. Some have relied on methods of inquiry and of data collection not typically or extensively used in the mental health field to validate ideas. Oral histories, historical documents, diaries, national and international policies and events, literary contributions (folktales and novels, for instance) by Asian and Pacific Americans, and introspection have formed the basis for some of the literature on personality, identity, and well-being.

The proliferation of different perspectives and of data collection has enriched the field. However, the Asian and Pacific American literature is still composed largely of critiques or criticisms of past works rather than of theory building or empirical tests of the validity of ideas. We believe that this problem is the result of underdevelopment rather than the fruitlessness of empirical research approaches. Instead of abandoning social science research in mental health, investigators should attempt to make more innovative and empirical contributions.

Despite the reservations that many individuals have over the possible detrimental consequences of research findings, as mentioned earlier, Asian American mental health research will continue to play a necessary role in the promotion of the welfare of these peoples. Data on the numbers of Asian and Pacific Americans, their characteristics and needs, stress conditions, resources, cultural patterns, psychological disturbance, and the outcome of intervention efforts are vital. Decision makers are interested in and influenced by high-quality research even when it challenges the political status quo or conventional wisdom (Weiss and Weiss, 1981).

Directions for Improved Research

What directions should mental health research take? This question deals with an evaluation of priorities: a determination of the kinds of research that are most helpful, important, beneficial, or meaningful. Such a task is difficult, since consensus may not exist. The Asian/Pacific American Subpanel of the President's Commission on Mental Health (1978) made a large number of recommendations for research, including the following:

1. Investigating ongoing racism and its effects on Asian and Pacific American communities.
2. Studying normative patterns of functioning among and within these communities.

3. Remedying information gaps, especially those related to census information, population status, service utilization patterns, and service needs.
4. Researching particular groups, such as women, children, refugees, rural and urban populations, Pacific Island communities, the developmentally disabled population, and the Asian wives of United States servicemen.
5. Identifying the kinds of services available.
6. Developing culturally appropriate and relevant psychological assessment tools.
7. Investigating family functioning and configurations.
8. Developing, implementing and evaluating prevention programs.
9. Assessing the role of informal cultural supportive networks as possible preventive and therapeutic resources.

Judging from these recommendations, the subpanel apparently wanted to make broad rather than specific suggestions, to emphasize the lack of even the most basic descriptive data (for example, census and population information), and to emphasize the need for research in assessment and intervention.

Sue, Ito, and Bradshaw (1982) have also tried to specify directions for research in all areas involving Asian and Pacific Americans. They propose a four-stage cycle of research (see Figure 2): (1) the status of Asian and Pacific Americans, (2) the causes of psychological well-being or disturbance, (3) solutions to mental health problems, and (4) implementation of solutions. These four areas are intimately related. Without knowledge of the status and well-being of Asian and Pacific Americans, it is fruitless to look for causal factors for problems. In the absence of knowledge of cause or etiology, then it is exceedingly difficult to plan for solutions. Finally, knowing the solutions to problems is of no value unless the solutions can be implemented in policies and programs, which in turn influence the status and well-being of Asian and Pacific Americans.

Research on Status. Basic demographic and epidemiological information on Asian and Pacific Americans is needed. Because of methodological, conceptual, and practical problems in

Figure 2. Four-Stage Cycle of Research.

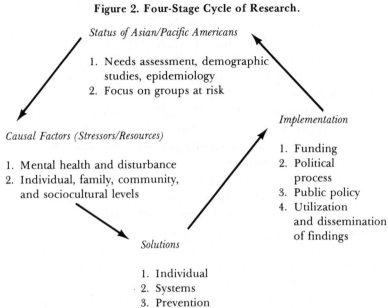

Status of Asian/Pacific Americans

1. Needs assessment, demographic
   studies, epidemiology
2. Focus on groups at risk

Implementation

1. Funding
2. Political
   process
3. Public policy
4. Utilization
   and dissemination
   of findings

Causal Factors (Stressors/Resources)

1. Mental health and disturbance
2. Individual, family, community,
   and sociocultural levels

Solutions

1. Individual
2. Systems
3. Prevention

Source: Sue, Ito, and Bradshaw, 1982; Copyright 1982 by Praeger Publishers. Reprinted by permission of Praeger Publishers.

ethnic research, accurate information is lacking. Controversy continues to exist on the sizes of various Asian and Pacific American groups, on their geographical locations, and on the extent of mental disorders, drug abuse, and alcoholism. Information of this kind is essential if appropriate programs and policies are to be developed. Furthermore, the status of groups believed to be at particular risk for mental health problems should be ascertained and receive high priority in research investigations. Immigrants, the poor, and the elderly may be among the high-risk groups. Hinkle (1974) has shown that immigrants are exposed to enormous life changes requiring personal readjustment. These changes are highly related to the incidence of physical and psychological problems. Research has also consistently shown a negative correlation between social class and psychopathology (Dohrenwend and Dohrenwend, 1974a). For Asian Americans, a race by social class interaction may further exacerbate psychological well-being. To the extent that the interaction exists, one cannot demonstrate its existence by studying a race or social class variable alone. More sophisticated designs with larger numbers of subjects are needed to explore the interaction effect. The same may be true for the elderly, who encounter the same problems with aging as do all Americans. In this case, however, factors associated with minority group status may be implicated.

Research on Etiology. What are the causal factors that affect the status of Asian and Pacific Americans? Psychological well-being is a function of having positive mental health *and* not having mental disturbance. Mental health includes topics such as self-esteem, self-identity, happiness, achievement, and feelings of mastery and control. Mental disturbance encompasses what are traditionally considered psychopathological disorders (for example, personality disorders, schizophrenia, or drug abuse).

From the perspective adopted in this book, mental health and disturbance are influenced by stressors and resources. While social scientists have largely studied such stressors as culture conflict, culture shock, stereotypes, discrimination, poverty, and life changes, growing interest has emerged in the effects of social networks. Networks refer to the interpersonal contacts available in one's family, neighborhood, community, culture, and society. As indicated in Chapter Four, networks can enhance or detract from psychological well-being.

Research on Solutions. Knowledge of the factors that affect psychological well-being must somehow be utilized in the development of solutions. The knowledge, for example, that life changes can create stress does not enable us to develop concrete intervention programs. We still need to know how to reduce life changes for immigrants or to prepare them for developing better coping strategies. Fairweather and his colleagues (Fairweather, Sanders, and Tornatzky, 1974) have tried to emphasize how research can be used to find solutions to problems. Their approach is to create innovative programs that can be shown to be more effective than currently used programs, which may be harmful or unresponsive. The elements in their process of experimental social innovation include (1) defining the problem to be addressed by obtaining feedback from the target population, by reviewing published literature, and by naturalistic observations; (2) proposing different solutions to the problem; (3) experimentally testing the adequacy of the proposed solutions in the community; (4) assessing outcomes over time; (5) selecting the best solution, and (6) implementing the best solution. In this procedure, new and more useful solutions to problems may be found.

In the search for solutions, efforts can be directed toward the level of intervention, the type of intervention (mainstream versus ethnic), and the time of intervention.

The level of intervention refers to whether solutions are directed toward individual, group, systems, or societal levels. In clinical psychology, individuals and groups comprise the typical domain for intervention. Research into therapist, client, and situational factors that are associated with positive therapeutic outcomes is included in clinical solutions. Such research is important because of the mismatch between mental health practices and the low utilization, premature termination, and poor outcomes shown by clients from the various Asian/Pacific American groups. At a higher level, and one typically examined by the field of community psychology, one is concerned with the involvement of institutional, systemic, and societal solutions. From this perspective, mental health varies as a function of the practices, policies, and structure of the institutions and systems in society. For example, findings that the rate of mental disturbance is higher in disorganized communities, where there is greater crime, poverty, underemployment, and anonymity than in organized communities, are interpreted as reflecting the increased stressors and lowered resources found in disorganized communities. While there is evidence that disturbed persons "drift" or locate into disorganized communities, the very conditions of these communities also foster disturbance. The level of intervention is aimed at the social structure. For Asian and Pacific Americans, attempts to reduce stressors might take the form of combating prejudice and discrimination, eliminating racial stereotypes in the mass media, or reducing the poverty, unemployment, or poor housing conditions that may be found in certain Asian and Pacific American communities. Community service agencies or programs may be coordinated or created to provide effective resources. Newcomer or orientation programs for immigrants, use of ethnic churches to assist individuals, coordination of community institutions, and organizing mental health agencies to deal with culturally diverse clients may be some of the appropriate mechanisms to improve the mental health of individuals at a community level.

Another consideration in the search for solutions to mental health problems is the type of intervention. Asian Americans may have historical or culturally determined means of dealing with problems. More adequate solutions, then, may be derived from the mainstream mental health system or from the ethnic culture. Certain patterns of obtaining aid—for example, by using herbalists, relatives, third-party intermediaries, physicians, or church leaders—may be more common among Asian/Pacific Americans than other Americans. If this is the case, then it would be important to discover the range, utilization, and effectiveness of these cultural resources. Enhancement of such resources or their integration with traditional mental health services can then be explored.

Finally, the time of intervention is important. In the search for programs that enhance mental health, research and intervention have more often than not focused on treatment or remediation. Intervention occurs after an emotional problem or personal difficulty arises. In contrast, primary prevention programs intervene *before* the possible onset of emotional disturbance. Such programs attempt to reduce the incidence (new cases) of a disorder during a specified time period for a particular population. For example, if 1 percent of a population develops schizophrenia each year and a primary prevention program is initiated, a significant reduction in the 1 percent rate would suggest that the program is effective (assuming that no other factors are responsible for the rate decrease). Primary prevention is accomplished in three ways: (1) elimination or reduction of stressors that contribute to a disorder; (2) building of resources that allow individuals to cope or adapt; and (3) isolation of causal factors from individuals. Thus, research programs to evaluate the effectiveness of primary prevention are important. The Asian and Pacific American Subpanel to the President's Commission on Mental Health (1978) strongly urged the initiation of such programs.

Other prevention strategies are also possible, although they do not reduce the incidence of disorders. In secondary prevention, the prevalence (that is, the new and existing cases of a disorder during a specified time period for a particular population) rate is reduced. Through early detection and prompt treatment, the duration of a disorder can be reduced, thereby decreasing the prevalence rate. Community education programs that alert Asian and Pacific Americans to recognize emotional disturbance and that indicate sources of assistance for troubled individuals may enable the individuals to overcome their difficulties more rapidly. Lastly, tertiary prevention occurs when individuals recovering from emotional disturbance are rehabilitated or are reintegrated into community life. In all prevention efforts, research is necessary to discover directions for intervention and to evaluate the fruits of such efforts.

Research on Implementation. Unfortunately, even if knowledge about effective programs or solutions is acquired, the implementation of the knowledge is a different issue altogether. The former involves knowing what to do; the latter involves the actualization of the knowledge (that is, the "doing"). It would be a far easier task if research played a strong role in determining programs and policies. The battlefield for implementation of programs would be the research arena, where issues could be studied and analyzed. However, as Sarason (1976) has recognized, researchers who attempt to secure funding must often conform to federal guidelines, which may not focus on the most important arenas to research. Similarly, Fairweather (1972) discovered that decision makers often fail to implement programs that can be shown to be more effective and cost-beneficial than the currently existing programs. In his research, Fairweather found that chronic schizophrenic patients functioned more productively when they were given autonomy and experience in the community instead of being confined in hospitals. The problem was that hospitals were not willing to adopt the autonomy program. How does one convince administrators to implement a program that has proved effective?

Fairweather attempted to answer that question. By studying whom to contact (entry), what kinds of tactics are persuasive (message), and how to put the program into actions (implementation), he gained insight into the processes involved in the actualization of solutions.

It has been argued that research should be undertaken into the early phases of the policy process. That is, it is necessary to know the relationship between psychological research and the development of political influence, legislation, and decision making, all of which may have an impact on the implementation of programs and solutions. Individuals often do not adopt new or innovative programs for a number of reasons. Desires to maintain control or the status quo, uncertainty on how the programs will be received, fears over risk taking, and concern over the economic and political implications of implementing new programs or solutions for problems may be important sources of resistance.

The lessons learned from the ideas of Fairweather and others are clear. If Asian and Pacific Americans are to implement solutions that promote their welfare, they should find out —through research—how to influence program planners and decision makers. Specifically, they should find ways to convey to policy makers that Asian Americans are not model minority groups and that service programs must take into account linguistic and cultural traditions.

Sometimes, of course, effective solutions cannot be implemented because individuals in the community may fail to participate. Suppose, for example, that a team of bilingual and bicultural therapists has developed an effective treatment program for Asian and Pacific American clients and that the program organizers have persuaded decision makers to fund and initiate the treatment program on a permanent basis. In one sense, a solution and its implementation have been achieved. However, the solution is viable only if consumers utilize the program. A good program with adequate funding, resources, and personnel can wither if it is not used. In Chapter Two we indicated that Brown and his associates (1973) developed a psychiatric program for Chinese Americans in Chinatown, Los Angeles. Even after services were offered free of charge, no new clients were seen. Therefore, although social scientists have directed their energies toward decision makers in trying to implement programs, attention must also be paid to the people the programs are intended to serve. Research into how programs are accepted by individuals as well as what techniques are useful in increasing consumer participation is important. This must be used in conjunction with already identified goals of affecting policies through social and political influence, persuasion, and the increase of Asian American participation as administrators, members of review group panels, and policy makers.

Research Methodology

In obtaining knowledge, researchers have at their disposal a variety of techniques. As mentioned earlier in this chapter, because of the multidisciplinary interest and the paucity of empirical research, many investigators have relied on historical documents and archival materials, diaries, literary works, and introspection to generate and test ideas and theories. The mental health profession and the field of psychology have traditionally relied on several modes of inquiry. Table 12 shows some of the more common methods. Several are not mutually exclusive. For instance, an experimental approach can be in the form of a simulation.

When little is known about a group, researchers often rely on personal observations, correlational studies, and case studies as a means of acquiring basic information. As data accumulate and as hypotheses and theories are generated, other methods —most notably, experiments and simulations—are increasingly used as investigators try to determine cause-effect relationships.

As mentioned earlier, most of the literature on Asian and Pacific Americans consists of reports based on personal observations or correlational studies. More sophisticated methods have rarely been used because, among other reasons, investigators have encountered problems in finding valid measures with which to study Asian and Pacific Americans. How can tools be devised that adequately measure the attitudes, behaviors, and

Table 12. Commonly Used Research Methods.

Method	Process
1. Observation	Watching or taking notes of an event or phenomenon. Observer may rely on personal judgment and memory or use rigorous and well-controlled procedures to record an event.
2. Correlation	Determining the degree of relationship between two or more variables.
3. Experiment	Manipulating an independent variable to note its effects on a dependent variable.
4. Simulation	Creating under controlled conditions a study that as closely as possible replicates a real-life situation.
5. Field Study	Observing phenomena as they occur naturally in the environment.
6. Single-Subject Study	Using an experimental approach to study the behavior of one person.
7. Case Study	Using observations, psychological tests, historical data, and biographical information to study one person.

characteristics of Asian and Pacific Americans? The reduction of culture bias, control of response sets, and correct interpretation of findings are major tasks.

Brislin, Lonner, and Thorndike (1973) outline various means suggested by researchers to reduce culture bias in tests. The first method is to construct tests equally unfamiliar to all cultures. In practice, this method is virtually impossible because tests are designed within particular cultural settings and the designers consciously or unconsciously use many cultural requisites in the development of their tests.

Second, one can use culturally appropriate tests or tasks, whereby a particular psychological dimension is assessed by means of a medium familiar to the members of each culture. In intelligence testing, Williams (1975) has advocated culture-specific tests for Blacks. Arguing that most IQ tests are culturally specific—that is, designed for and normalized on White, middle-class culture—he has developed the Black Intelligence Test of Cultural Homogeneity, which presumably taps more of Black culture. On this test, Blacks score higher than Whites. Sample multiple-choice items from a version of the test are (correct answers underlined): (1) to "get down" means: to dominate; to travel; to lower a position; or <u>to have sexual intercourse</u>; (2) "cop" an attitude means: leave; <u>become angry</u>; sit down; protect a neighborhood. It is not difficult to develop tests on which one culture does well while other cultures do poorly. The key issues are whether culture-specific tests are each measuring the same attributes (in this case, intelligence) and whether cross-cultural comparisons are meaningful. These two key issues are still being debated.

The American Psychological Association (APA) has been investigating the problem of culture bias in intelligence testing. In a letter to the APA Board of Directors, dated October 26, 1978, the APA Board of Professional Affairs acknowledged that any test is subject to some kind of cultural bias and to misuse; however, the degree and extent of bias, the practical effect of the presumed bias, and the inherent undesirability of the bias are open to question. Moreover, if means other than intelligence tests—for example, criterion-referenced tests (in which the teacher takes the responsibility for placing students in special classes)—are used to predict future performance and to place students in special education programs, greater bias may be introduced. In other words, the board asked what alternatives are available, in view of the necessity to evaluate and predict student performance and to appropriately place students in programs that maximally benefit students according to their abilities. Although these concerns are over intelligence testing, they raise similar issues for the assessment of mental health. Culture bias, predictive validity, culture-specific tests, and alternative assessment procedures are relevant to the evaluation of mental health. There are obviously many unresolved issues in the use of culturally specific tests.

A third possible method of reducing culture bias is to balance the use of tests in different cultures. Develop test A in Culture A for use in Cultures A and B. Develop test B in Culture B for use in Cultures A and B. Thus, both cultures receive tests A and B. By counterbalancing the order of presentation of the tests to each culture, any bias from test administration conditions can cancel out. Procedurally, this technique seems to be the "fairest"; the problem is, of course, to see that the tests developed in cultures A and B are tapping the same attribute.

Finally, one can use the same test but apply relative rules for performance of diverse cultural groups. According to Brislin and his associates, it is not the internal item-by-item fairness features or the scores alone that are important. What are important are the uses to which test scores are put (for example, personnel selection, educational placement, or psychotherapeutic treatment decisions). For example, fairness can be developed by setting levels of test performance that will qualify applicants or students from different cultural groups in proportion to the percentage of those in the groups who reach a specified level of criterion performance. Different regression formulas would be developed for each group, with the formulas related to the same levels of criterion performance across groups. This procedure accepts the universality of the test as an assessment instrument but recognizes the relativity of mean test scores between cultures. It does not, however, deal with the possibility that a test that may be valid (measuring what it purports to measure) for one culture may not be for another. Mercer (1971) has shown that IQ tests are "Anglocentric"—that is, they measure the extent to which an individual's background matches the average cultural pattern of White American society. In her study, Blacks and Hispanics had lower average IQ scores than Whites. However, IQ scores for the Blacks and Hispanics were directly related to the degree that their families possessed Anglo characteristics (in social, occupational, and other demographic factors). Those whose families shared a large number of characteristics with the average White family had IQs equal to those of White children. The IQ test, then, may well be able to predict academic and occupational success in this country, but as a measure of general intelligence, especially for members of different cultures, its use is questionable if the tests are more a measure of socialization to a specific culture and even if separate norms are developed for each culture.

Summary

Many individuals have been critical of research on Asian and Pacific Americans. They argue, for example, that research is too theoretical to be of applied value or that research intrinsically cannot enhance the welfare of Asian Americans. Contrary to these views, research on the whole, whether theoretical or applied, does have important impact on policies and programs. The impact can be positive or negative. For example, research that presents inaccurate or culturally biased information can be detrimental. We suggest that researchers form close and collaborative relationships with Asian and Pacific American communities to maximize the beneficial effects of research with these communities.

Unfortunately, mental health research is still at an elementary stage. The validity of typically used measures is unknown, appreciation of studying Asian Americans is lacking, and most research is relatively unsophisticated and not designed to test theories. Needed are studies examining individual differences and groups other than Chinese and Japanese Americans. Encouraging more Asian and Pacific American researchers and different and more sophisticated empirical approaches would also be beneficial.

Particular areas that need researching include research on the status of Asian and Pacific Americans, the causes of mental health and disturbance, solutions, and the implementation of solutions. Greater attention also should be given to empirical research approaches and to the construction of valid psychological measures.

8

Future Directions
for Helping
Asian Americans

Our intent in this book has
been to assess and critically evaluate current knowledge on
Asian and Pacific American mental health by examining critical
areas such as the nature and rate of mental disturbance, the expression of symptoms, family dynamics, personality, treatment
and intervention, and research. In evaluating these areas, we
have stressed the notions of culture and cultural relativism, person-environment match, minority group experiences and history,
and a diasthesis-stressor-resource model of well-being.

Major Findings

Before we elaborate on the implications and make extrap-
olations, let us review the major findings.

1. Rates of mental disorders among Asian and Pacific
Americans have been underestimated. Although the treated-case
method of determining rates shows a significant underutilization

of mental health services, the appropriateness of this method can be questioned. Cultural values as well as difficulties in finding responsive services—factors unrelated to rates of disturbance—seem largely responsible for the underutilization. The most valid means of ascertaining the rates of disorders, the untreated-case method, has not been employed with Asian and Pacific Americans.

2. The expression of symptoms is influenced by culture. Many Asian/Pacific Americans exhibit somatic complaints along with feelings of anger, frustration, anxiety, and depression.

3. Because of racism, exposure to contrasting cultures and life-styles, and rapid social changes, Asian Americans are experiencing stress. The available data and the observations of contemporary social scientists do not corroborate the view that Asian Americans are extraordinarily well adjusted. As would be expected, certain groups—such as immigrants, refugees, the elderly, and women—are at particular risk.

4. Many social scientists have used family processes and role structures to explain the behavior and adaptation of Asian/Pacific Americans. Although the strengths of Asian/Pacific American families in adaptation have been stressed, the close family relationships and group-centered (as opposed to individualistic) orientation may also create interpersonal difficulties. Little research has been devoted to the role of family in preparing persons to live in a bicultural or multicultural environment.

5. Important philosophical differences have emerged in the interpretation of research findings in the area of personality and identity. Some researchers have attacked personality research for methodological and conceptual reasons. They believe that current research findings do not adequately convey the sensibilities of Asian and Pacific Americans. The controversy highlights disagreements over the assessment and implications of bicultural characteristics and adaptation. Most research investigations have demonstrated a progressive assimilation into American society. Whether or not traditional studies of assimilation can capture the bicultural nature of Asian/Pacific Americans in personality, identity, and sex roles remain one of the major issues of contention.

6. In order to alleviate and prevent emotional disturbance, it is necessary to intervene at the levels of psychotherapy, system change, and community empowerment. Successful intervention approaches for Asian Americans should involve consideration of the bilingual and bicultural backgrounds that these peoples often possess, the match between intervention tactics and client or community, and experience in working with Asian and Pacific Americans.

7. Despite the cynicism by some Asian and Pacific Americans over the value of research in solving human problems, research is vital not only in providing new knowledge but also in developing programs and policies. The main problem is not the inability of research to yield policy-relevant findings; rather, the quality and quantity of research on Asian/Pacific Americans have been limited. In addition to descriptive and correlational studies, the formulation and testing of theories using a wide range of empirical methodologies that are employed in the social sciences are needed. The particular areas in the mental health field that are important to investigate include research on the status of Asian and Pacific Americans, the causal factors in mental health and disturbance, solutions, and means of implementing solutions. Funding opportunities for research on Asian and Pacific Americans are also needed (Cheung, 1980; Kuramoto, 1976).

Future Directions

After reviewing the mental health literature, one can easily have mixed feelings over the accumulated knowledge on Asian and Pacific Americans. There are certainly enough theoretical contributions and empirical studies with which to generate new and exciting studies. The knowledge base is sufficient for serious students of Asian and Pacific Americans to conduct more than mere descriptive investigations and to develop a specialty on these groups. For example, Hurh, Kim, and Kim (1978) and Kuo (1976) have used various Asian American populations to make empirical tests of theories. On the other hand, the mental health work primarily serves to whet the appetite rather than to provide a substantial meal. There are major disagreements concerning the means to conceptualize Asian and Pacific American personality, mental health, and identity; the kinds of research strategies and tools that best capture and describe the sensibilities of Asian Americans; and the methods to intervene effectively. Rather than to simply state that more research is needed, we will indicate some of the directions for research and some broad implications concerning Asian/Pacific Americans.

Many of the issues confronting Asian and Pacific Americans (and ethnic minority groups in general) challenge fundamental values and principles held in psychology and American society. To see how this occurs, let us examine the notion of paradox.

Rappaport (1981) and McGrath (1980) believe that many issues facing behavioral scientists and practitioners consist of paradoxes in which two or more positive or cherished values are pitted against one another. According to Rappaport, some paradoxes are false. While at first glance the values may appear contradictory, on closer examination they may not actually be self-contradictory. These false paradoxes can be resolved through convergent reasoning, in which different solutions are proposed and converge on the "right" answer. In principle, a solution can be found. In the case of "real" paradoxes or antimonies, two or more laws, principles, or ideals are in reality contradictory. For example, freedom of expression or speech often clashes with one's perceived right to be protected from unwanted or harmful materials. Under the principle of freedom of expression, should one have a right to expose others to pornographic materials? Should one have a right to expose others to racial slurs? Should one have a right to expose others to sexist values?

Several propositions can be drawn from antimonies or true paradoxes (Sue, 1981a). First, the strengthening of one principle or value generally weakens the contradictory principle. For instance, efforts to increase protection from unwanted materials limit the freedom of expression. Second, divergent rather than convergent reasoning is required in finding solutions, since the latter process obscures the inherent nature of the contradiction. That is, by trying to find *the* solution, one denies the legitimacy of the fundamental contradiction. Third, the important task is to identify true paradoxes and to propose a number of diverse solutions. These solutions may require change over time to meet new issues or challenges that evolve from the paradoxes.

In our examination of Asian and Pacific Americans, many of the issues discussed fall into three antimonies.

Etic Versus Emic. Who are Asian and Pacific Americans? What are their value systems, characteristics, and life-styles? The etic-emic antimony is relevant to such questions. The etic approach emphasizes the universal characteristics of human beings, regardless of cultural variations. The emic approach defines human characteristics as a function of culture and adopts a position of relativity rather than universality. The distinction is similar to the idiographic-nomothetic controversy in psychology. Both approaches are legitimate in the sense that human beings are alike in some respects and different in other respects. However, American psychology has traditionally opted for an etic perspective based on an Anglo model (Brislin, Lonner, and Thorndike, 1973). As a result, the etic is strengthened at the expense of the emic, and cultural relativity has gone largely unappreciated. By providing more of an emic perspective, we have attempted to illustrate the importance of cultural considerations in the personality, mental health, family patterns, and behaviors of Asian and Pacific Americans. Arguments were also presented to demonstrate the negative consequences of the etic approach in mental health treatment and intervention and in theory and research.

In illustrating the importance of culture, we are not asserting the greater legitimacy of the emic view. Such an assertion would deny the validity of antimony and would imply that the solution to understanding Asian and Pacific Americans entails simply increased knowledge of cultures. The danger in holding a completely emic perspective is that not all problems can be traced to cultural determinants. The important point is that solutions require a balance between the two legitimate perspectives rather than the dominance of one over the other.

At another level, the etic-emic is reflected in the use of the concept of modal personality. In studying groups, researchers often characterize a particular group by referring to the average or modal traits found in that group. For example, Asian and Pacific Americans are said to be deferent and/or family oriented because their modal pattern of traits exhibits these characteristics. By focusing on modal personalities, one neglects individual differences.

Mainstreaming Versus Pluralism. Related to the etic-emic struggle is one involving mainstreaming versus pluralism. The former values uniformity and adherence to the mainstream standards. Deviations from the dominant group norms are considered undesirable. Therefore, immigrants should learn English and adopt certain behavioral patterns, such as individualism, competition, and assertiveness, since these characteristics are functional in society. On the other hand, advocates of pluralism believe that diversity is desirable and that society should tolerate and respect the richness inherent in cultural differences.

The antimony involves a clash of fundamental values. How can one argue against the acquisition of functional skills and some degree of "Americanization"? Similarly, how can one doubt the necessity for respect and tolerance of cultural diversity in a country with a heritage of immigrants and a philosophy of freedom and democracy? The problem is that the mainstream view has been dominant. This dominance can be seen in two areas. First, as discussed in previous chapters, the mental health system has not been adequately flexible to deal with the kinds of problems presented by Asian and Pacific Americans. The underlying assumption is that people should change (if they are not in the mainstream) to meet the requirements of the mental health system. A pluralism perspective would emphasize the system changes that must take place to meet the diverse population. Second, the mainstreaming effort can also be seen in the stress on assimilation or Anglo-conformity (Gordon, 1978). While some degree of assimilation is necessary and inevitable, mainstreaming advocates often fail to appreciate potential side effects. Appeals for assimilation may implicitly undermine the respect for different cultural values, resulting in ethnocentrism for those in the mainstream and poor self-identity for those in the ethnic minority cultures. Furthermore, assimilation does not proceed uniformly, and some values that are adopted may be detrimental to the minority group. Yamamoto and Wagatsuma (1980) have noted some costs associated with the acculturation of Japanese Americans. For example, with increasing assimilation, the divorce rate may increase, and the values of group support, interdependency, and family integrity may decrease.

Equal Opportunity Versus Equality of Outcome. In attempts to foster equality, individuals have attempted to discover instances of discrimination or differential treatment on the basis of race or ethnicity. Early studies revealed that ethnic minority group clients did receive inferior and discriminatory forms of treatment (Yamamoto, James, and Palley, 1968). These findings initiated a movement to improve accessibility to services and equality of treatment. However, when opportunities for treatment were equalized, outcomes were not necessarily equalized. For example, Sue (1977a) found that even when ethnic minority clients received the same kinds of treatment and services as Whites in community mental health centers, they tended to have poorer outcomes. The problem is clear. Individuals who value equal treatment opportunities (that is, seeing that discrimination in services does not exist) may unwittingly perpetuate unequal outcomes; those who advocate equal outcomes (that is, seeing that minority groups are as likely as Whites to benefit from mental health services) may have to discriminate by treating some groups differently because of cultural differences.

In our discussion of Asian and Pacific Americans, problems in achieving equal outcomes from treatment have been highlighted. Particularly for those clients who markedly differ from mainstream Americans, some discriminatory treatment may be necessary. Such treatment, however, is intended to improve outcomes rather than to reflect racism, which inevitably results in poor outcomes.

The etic-emic, mainstreaming-pluralism, and equal opportunity-equal outcome controversies will become even more salient for Asian and Pacific Americans since these groups are becoming more diverse and noticeable and are increasing in numbers. Considering the large influx of immigrants and the social-political changes in the United States, new problems and issues emerge. Asian Americans will show even greater diversity. Newer groups, such as Korean and Southeast Asian American groups, are increasing rapidly in number; the recent immigrants (such as those from Hong Kong or Japan) may be in many ways quite Westernized compared to their immigrant counterparts of several generations ago (indeed, they may in some ways be more Westernized than second- and third-generation Chinese and Japanese Americans); the civil rights climate has changed, so that the struggles of immigrants in the late 1800s and early 1900s are likely to be different for new immigrants; changes in international affairs, such as the recognition of Mainland China as a potential ally and superpower, may well change the perception of many non-Asian Americans toward certain Asian Americans; the growing network of Asian and Pacific Americans provides resources that were not previously available; the presence of fifth- and sixth-generation Asian Americans and of new immigrants will raise even greater issues of group identity and solidarity; the presence of the children of interracial marriages will also raise major issues of group identity, acceptance, and solidarity; the discrepancy between the large numbers of the highly educated and upwardly mobile and of the minimally educated and poverty stricken may increase over time. These and other developments pose new challenges for the mental health profession and for American society.

References

Abbott, E. "Letter to the Editor." *Amerasia Journal,* 1973, *2,* 180-182.

Abbott, K. A. "Chinese-American Society." *Amerasia Journal,* 1972, *1,* 68-74.

Abbott, K. A. "Culture Change and the Persistence of the Chinese Personality." In G. DeVos (Ed.), *Responses to Change: Society, Culture, and Personality.* New York: Van Nostrand, 1976.

Abbott, K. A., and Abbott, E. L. "Juvenile Delinquency in San Francisco's Chinese-American Community: 1961-1966." *Journal of Sociology,* 1968, *4,* 45-56.

Albee, G. W. "A Competency Model to Replace the Deficit Model." In M. S. Gibbs, J. R. Lachenmayer, and J. Sigal (Eds.), *Community Psychology: Theoretical and Empirical Approaches.* New York: Gardner Press, 1980.

Alcantara, R. R. *The Filipinos in Hawaii: An Annotated Bibliography.* Honolulu: Social Sciences and Linguistics Institute, University of Hawaii, 1977.

Allport, G. W. *The Nature of Prejudice.* Reading, Mass.: Addison-Wesley, 1954.

Arkoff, A. "Need Patterns in Two Generations of Japanese Americans in Hawaii." *Journal of Social Psychology,* 1959, *50,* 75-79.

Arkoff, A., Meredith, G., and Dong, J. "Attitudes of Japanese-American and Caucasian-American Students Toward Marriage Roles." *Journal of Social Psychology,* 1963, *59,* 11-15.

Arkoff, A., Meredith, G., and Iwahara, S. "Dominance-Deference Patterns in Motherland Japanese, Japanese-Americans, and Caucasian-American Students." *Journal of Social Psychology,* 1962, *58,* 61-66.

Arkoff, A., Thaver, F., and Elkind, L. "Mental Health and Counseling Ideas of Asian and American Students." *Journal of Counseling Psychology,* 1966, *13,* 219-223.

Arkoff, A., and Weaver, H. "Body Image and Body Dissatisfaction in Japanese-Americans." *Journal of Social Psychology,* 1966, *68,* 323-330.

"Asian Women as Leaders." *Rodan* (Northern California Asian American Community News), April 1971.

Atkinson, D. R., Maruyama, M., and Matsui, S. "The Effects of Counselor Race and Counseling Approach on Asian Americans' Perceptions of Counselor Credibility and Utility." *Journal of Counseling Psychology,* 1978, *25,* 76-83.

Attneave, C. "Mental Health of American Indians: Problems, Perspectives, and Challenge for the Decade Ahead." Paper presented at meeting of the American Psychological Association, Honolulu, Aug. 1972.

Ayabe, H. I. "Deference and Ethnic Differences in Voice Levels." *Journal of Social Psychology,* 1971, *85,* 181-185.

Aylesworth, L. S., Ossorio, P. G., and Osaki, L. T. "Stress and Mental Health Among Vietnamese in the United States." In R. Endo, S. Sue, and N. N. Wagner (Eds.), *Asian Americans: Social and Psychological Perspectives.* Palo Alto, Calif.: Science and Behavior Books, 1980.

Ball, J. C., and Lau, M. P. "The Chinese Narcotic Addict in the United States." *Social Forces,* 1966, *45,* 68-72.

Banks, W. C., and others. "Perceived Objectivity and Effects of Evaluative Reinforcement upon Compliance and Self-Evaluation in Blacks." *Journal of Experimental Social Psychology,* 1977, *13,* 452-463.

Barnett, M. L., "Alcoholism in the Cantonese of New York City: An Anthropological Study." In O. Diethelm (Ed.), *Etiology of Chronic Alcoholism.* Springfield, Ill.: Thomas, 1955.

Berk, B. B., and Hirata, L. C. "Mental Illness Among the Chinese: Myth or Reality?" *Journal of Social Issues,* 1973, *29,* 149-166.

Bernal, M. E., and Padilla, A. M. "Status of Minority Curricula and Training in Clinical Psychology: 1980." *American Psychologist,* in press.

Bloom, B. L. *Community Mental Health: A General Introduction.* Monterey, Calif.: Brooks/Cole, 1977.

Bogardus, E. S. *Immigration and Race Attitudes.* Boston: Heath, 1928.

Bourne, P. G. "Suicide Among Chinese in San Francisco." *American Journal of Public Health,* 1973, *63,* 744-750.

Bourne, P. G. "The Chinese Student—Acculturation and Mental Illness." *Psychiatry,* 1975, *38,* 269-277.

Bradburn, N. *The Structure of Psychological Well-Being.* Hawthorne, N.Y.: Aldine, 1970.

Brazziel, W. F. "White Research in Black Communities: When Solutions Become a Part of the Problem." *Journal of Social Issues,* 1973, *29,* 41-44.

Brigham, J. C. "Ethnic Stereotypes." *Psychological Bulletin,* 1971, *76,* 15-38.

Brislin, R. W., Lonner, W. J., and Thorndike, R. M. *Cross-Cultural Research Methods.* New York: Wiley, 1973.

Brown, B. S. "Foreword." In Conference Report Committee, *The First National Conference on Asian American Mental Health.* Washington, D.C.: U.S. Government Printing Office, 1974.

Brown, T. R., and others. "Mental Illness and the Role of Mental Health Facilities in Chinatown." In S. Sue and N. Wagner (Eds.), *Asian Americans: Psychological Perspectives.* Palo Alto, Calif.: Science and Behavior Books, 1973.

Callao, M. J. "Culture Shock: West, East, and West Again." *Personnel and Guidance Journal,* 1973, *51,* 413-416.

Cambra, R. E., Klopf, D. W., and Oka, B. J. *Communication Apprehension Among University of Hawaii Students.* Honolulu: Department of Speech, University of Hawaii, 1978. (Mimeographed.)

Campbell, D. T. "Stereotypes and the Perception of Group Differences." *American Psychologist,* 1967, *22,* 817-829.

Caplan, G. "Support Systems." Keynote address to the conference of the Department of Psychiatry, Rutgers Medical School, and the New Jersey Mental Health Association, Newark, 1972.

Caudill, W., and DeVos, G. "Achievement, Culture, and Personality: The Case of the Japanese-Americans." *American Anthropologist,* 1956, *58,* 1102-1126.

Cheung, F. K. "Mental Health Status of Asian Americans." *Clinical Psychologist,* 1980, *34,* 23-24.

Chin, R. "Conceptual Paradigm for a Racial-Ethnic Community: The Case of the Chinese American Community." In S. Sue and T. Moore (Eds.), *The Pluralistic Society: A Community Mental Health Perspective.* New York: Human Sciences Press, 1982.

Chu, G. "Drinking Patterns and Attitudes of Rooming-House Chinese in San Francisco." *Quarterly Journal of Studies of Alcohol,* 1972, Supp., *6,* 58-68.

Chu, J. "Anna May Wong." In E. Gee (Ed.), *Counterpoint: Perspectives on Asian America.* Los Angeles: Asian American Studies Center, 1977.

Conference Report Committee. *The First National Conference on Asian American Mental Health.* Washington, D.C.: U.S. Government Printing Office, 1974.

Connor, J. W. "Acculturation and Changing Need Patterns in Japanese-American and Caucasian-American College Students." *Journal of Social Psychology,* 1974a, *93,* 293-294.

Connor, J. W. "Acculturation and Family Continuities in Three Generations of Japanese-Americans." *Journal of Marriage and the Family,* 1974b, *36,* 159-165.

Cordova, D. "Filipino American Community Issues." Paper presented at the National Endowment for the Humanities Conference, Seattle, June 1974.

DeVos, G. "Selective Permeability and Reference Group Sanctioning: Psychological Continuities in Role Degradation." Paper presented at seminar on Comparative Studies in Ethnicity and Nationality, University of Washington, Seattle, 1978.

Diamond, M. J., and Bond, M. H. "The Acceptance of 'Barnum' Personality Interpretations by Japanese, Japanese-American, and Caucasian-American Students." *Journal of Cross-Cultural Psychology,* 1974, *5,* 228-235.

Dohrenwend, B. P., and Dohrenwend, B. S. *Social Status and Psychological Disorder: A Causal Inquiry.* New York: Wiley, 1969.

Dohrenwend, B. P., and Dohrenwend, B. S. "Social and Cultural Influences on Psychopathology." *Annual Review of Psychology,* 1974a, *25,* 417-452.

Dohrenwend, B. S., and Dohrenwend, B. P. (Eds.). *Stressful Life Events: Their Nature and Effects.* New York: Wiley, 1974b.

Doi, M. L., Lin, C., and Vohra-Sahu, I. *Pacific/Asian American Research: An Annotated Bibliography.* Chicago: Pacific/Asian American Mental Health Research Center, 1981.

Dollard, J., and others. *Frustration and Aggression.* New Haven, Conn.: Yale University Press, 1939.

Dong, T., and others. "National Asian American Psychology Training Conference." *American Psychologist,* 1978, *33,* 691-692.

Duff, D. F., and Arthur, R. J. "Between Two Worlds: Filipinos in the U.S. Navy." *American Journal of Psychiatry,* 1967, *123,* 836-843.

Endo, R. "Whither Ethnic Studies: A Re-Examination of Some Issues." In S. Sue and N. Wagner (Eds.), *Asian-Americans: Psychological Perspectives.* Palo Alto, Calif.: Science and Behavior Books, 1973.

Enright, J. B., and Jaeckle, W. R. "Psychiatric Symptoms and Diagnosis in Two Subcultures." *International Journal of Social Psychiatry,* 1963, *9,* 12-17.

Ewalt, J. R. "The Birth of the Community Mental Health Movement." In W. Barton and C. Sanborn (Eds.), *An Assessment of the Mental Health Movement.* Lexington, Ky.: Lexington Books, 1977.

Ewing, J. A., Rouse, B. A., and Pellizzari, E. D. "Alcohol Sensitivity and Ethnic Background." *American Journal of Psychiatry,* 1974, *131,* 206-210.

Fairweather, G. W. *Social Change: The Challenge to Survival.* Morristown, N.J.: General Learning Press, 1972.

Fairweather, G. W., Sanders, D. H., and Tornatzky, L. G. *Creating Change in Mental Health Organizations.* Elmsford, N.Y.: Pergamon Press, 1974.

Fenz, W. D., and Arkoff, A. "Comparative Need Patterns of Five Ancestry Groups in Hawaii." *Journal of Social Psychology,* 1962, *58,* 67-89.

Finney, J. C. "Psychiatry and Multi-Culturality in Hawaii." *International Journal of Social Psychiatry,* 1963, *9,* 5-11.

Fong, S. L. M. "Assimilation of Chinese in America: Changes in Orientation and Social Perception." *American Journal of Sociology,* 1965, *71,* 265-273.

Fong, S. L. M. "Assimilation and Changing Social Roles of Chinese Americans." *Journal of Social Issues,* 1973, *29,* 115-127.

Fong, S. L. M., and Peskin, H. "Sex-Role Strain and Personality Adjustment of China-Born Students in America: A Pilot Study." *Journal of Abnormal Psychology,* 1969, *74,* 563-567.

Fujii, S. M. "Elderly Asian Americans and Use of Public Services." In R. Endo, S. Sue, and N. N. Wagner (Eds.), *Asian Americans: Social and Psychological Perspectives.* Palo Alto, Calif.: Science and Behavior Books, 1980.

Fujiki, R. E. "Strategies for Political Participation of Asian/ Pacific Women." In U.S. Commission on Civil Rights (Ed.), *Civil Rights Issues of Asian and Pacific Americans: Myths and Realities.* Washington, D.C.: U.S. Government Printing Office, 1980.

Fujitomi, I., and Wong, D. "The New Asian-American Woman." In S. Sue and N. Wagner (Eds.), *Asian-Americans: Psychological Perspectives.* Palo Alto, Calif.: Science and Behavior Books, 1973.

Gallimore, R., Weiss, L. B., and Finney, R. "Cultural Differences in Delay of Gratification: A Problem of Behavior Classification." *Journal of Personality and Social Psychology,* 1974, *30,* 72-80.

Garfield, S. L. *Clinical Psychology: The Study of Personality and Behavior.* Hawthorne, N.Y.: Aldine, 1974.

Gilbert, G. M. "Stereotype Persistence and Change Among College Students." *Journal of Abnormal and Social Psychology,* 1951, *46,* 245-254.

Gordon, M. M. *Human Nature, Class, and Ethnicity.* New York: Oxford University Press, 1978.

Grinder, R. E., and McMichael, R. E. "Cultural Influence on Conscience Development: Resistance to Temptation and Guilt Among Samoans and American Caucasians." *Journal of Abnormal and Social Psychology,* 1963, *66,* 503-507.

Gurin, G., Veroff, J., and Feld, S. *Americans View Their Mental Health.* New York: Basic Books, 1960.

Harris, T. "Asian American Enrollment Increases at UC Berkeley." *East/West,* 1981, *15,* 6-7.

Heer, D. M. "The Prevalence of Black-White Marriage in the United States, 1960 and 1970." *Journal of Marriage and the Family,* 1974, *36,* 246-258.

Hessler, R. M., and others. "Intraethnic Diversity: Health Care of the Chinese Americans." *Human Organization,* 1975, *34,* 253-262.

Hinkle, L. E. "The Effect of Exposure to Culture Change, Social Change, and Changes in Interpersonal Relationships on Health." In B. S. Dohrenwend and B. P. Dohrenwend (Eds.), *Stressful Life Events: Their Nature and Effects.* New York: Wiley, 1974.

Hirabayashi, J. "Nisei: The Quiet American?—A Re-Evaluation." *Amerasia Journal,* 1975, *3,* 114-129.

Hirano, I. "Poverty and Social Service Perspectives." In U.S. Commission on Civil Rights (Ed.), *Civil Rights Issues of Asian and Pacific Americans: Myths and Realities.* Washington, D.C.: U.S. Government Printing Office, 1980.

Hirata, L. C. "Research for What? Beyond Needs Assessment Research." In A. K. Murata and J. Salvador-Burris (Eds.), *Issues in Community Research: Asian American Perspectives.* Chicago: Pacific/Asian Mental Health Research Center, 1980.

Hobbs, N. "Sources of Gain in Psychotherapy." *American Psychologist,* 1962, *17,* 741-747.

Holmes, T. H., and Masuda, M. "Life Change and Illness Susceptibility." In B. S. Dohrenwend and B. P. Dohrenwend (Eds.), *Stressful Life Events: Their Nature and Effects.* New York: Wiley, 1974.

Houston, J. W. "Beyond Manzanar: A Personal View of Asian American Womanhood." In R. Endo, S. Sue, and N. N. Wagner (Eds.), *Asian Americans: Social and Psychological Perspectives*. Palo Alto, Calif.: Science and Behavior Books, 1980.

Hsieh, T. T. Y., Shybut, J., and Lotsof, E. J. "Internal Versus External Control and Ethnic Group Membership: A Cross-Cultural Comparison." *Journal of Consulting and Clinical Psychology*, 1969, *33*, 122-124.

Hsu, F. L. K. *Americans and Chinese*. New York: Doubleday, 1970.

Hsu, F. L. K. "Psychosocial Homeostasis and Jen: Conceptual Tools for Advancing Psychological Anthropology." *American Anthropologist*, 1971, *73*, 23-44.

Hsu, F. L. K. "Kinship Is the Key." *Center Magazine*, 1973, *6*, 4-14.

Hurh, W. M., Kim, H. C., and Kim, K. C. *Assimilation Patterns of Immigrants in the United States: A Case Study of Korean Immigrants in the Chicago Area*. Washington, D.C.: University Press of America, 1978.

Hutchinson, S., Arkoff, A., and Weaver, H. B. "Ethnic and Sex Factors in Classroom Responsiveness." *Journal of Social Psychology*, 1966, *69*, 321-325.

Indochinese Consultation Committee. *Report to the Alcohol, Drug Abuse and Mental Health Administration*. Washington, D.C.: Indochinese Consultation Committee, 1980. (Mimeographed.)

Inkeles, A., and Levinson, D. J. "National Character: The Study of Modal Personality and Sociocultural Systems." In G. Lindzey and E. Aronson (Eds.), *The Handbook of Social Psychology*. Reading, Mass.: Addison-Wesley, 1969.

Jahoda, M. *Current Concepts of Positive Mental Health*. New York: Basic Books, 1958.

Joint Commission on Mental Illness and Health. *Action for Mental Health*. New York: Wiley, 1961.

Jones, A., and Seagull, A. A. "Dimensions of the Relationship Between the Black Client and the White Therapist: A Theoretical Overview." *American Psychologist*, 1977, *32*, 850-855.

Kalish, R. A. "Suicide: An Ethnic Comparison in Hawaii." *Bulletin of Suicidology*, Dec. 1968, pp. 37-43.

Kalish, R. A., Maloney, M., and Arkoff, A. "Cross-Cultural

Comparisons of College Students' Marital-Role Preferences."
Journal of Social Psychology, 1966, *68*, 41-47.

Karlins, M., Coffman, T. L., and Walters, G. "On the Fading of
Social Stereotypes: Studies in Three Generations of College
Students." *Journal of Personality and Social Psychology*,
1969, *13*, 1-16.

Katz, D., and Braly, K. "Racial Stereotypes in One Hundred
College Students." *Journal of Abnormal and Social Psychology*, 1933, *28*, 280-290.

Kelly, J. G. "The Ecology of Social Support Systems: Foot-
notes to a Theory." Paper presented at the American Psychological Association convention, San Francisco, Aug. 1977.

Kikumura, A., and Kitano, H. H. L. "Interracial Marriage: A
Picture of the Japanese Americans." *Journal of Social Issues*,
1973, *29*, 67-81.

Kim, B. L. C. "Asian Wives of U.S. Servicemen: Women in
Shadows." *Amerasia Journal*, 1977, *4*, 91-115.

Kim, B. L. C. *The Asian Americans: Changing Patterns, Changing Needs*. Montclair, N.J.: Association of Korean Christian
Scholars in North America, 1978.

Kim, B. L. C. "Korean American Child at School and at Home."
Technical report to the Administration for Children, Youth,
and Families, Washington, D.C., 1980.

Kim, S. C. "The Utilization of Cultural Variables in the Training
of Clinical-Community Psychologists." *Journal of Community Psychology*, 1981, *9*, 298-300.

Kim, T. "Statement on Census Issues—Impact and Reaction."
In U.S. Commission on Civil Rights (Ed.), *Civil Rights Issues
of Asian and Pacific Americans: Myths and Realities*. Washington, D.C.: U.S. Government Printing Office, 1980.

Kitano, H. H. L. "Differential Child-Rearing Attitudes Between
First and Second Generation Japanese in the United States."
Journal of Social Psychology, 1961, *53*, 13-19.

Kitano, H. H. L. "Inter- and Intragenerational Differences in
Maternal Attitudes Toward Child Rearing." *Journal of Social
Psychology*, 1964, *63*, 215-220.

Kitano, H. H. L. "Japanese-American Crime and Delinquency."
Journal of Psychology, 1967, *66*, 253-263.

Kitano, H. H. L. "Japanese-American Mental Illness." In S. Plog and R. Edgerton (Eds.), *Changing Perspectives in Mental Illness.* New York: Holt, Rinehart and Winston, 1969.

Kitano, H. H. L. *Japanese Americans: The Evolution of a Subculture.* Englewood Cliffs, N.J.: Prentice-Hall, 1976.

Kitano, H. H. L. *Asian American Drinking Patterns.* Fourth Special Report to the Congress on Alcohol and Health. Washington, D.C.: Congress on Alcohol and Health, 1981.

Kitano, H. H. L., and Kikumura, A. "The Japanese American Family." In C. H. Mindel and R. W. Habenstein (Eds.), *Ethnic Families in America.* New York: Elsevier, 1976.

Kitano, H. H. L., and Yeung, W. "Chinese Interracial Marriage." *Journal of Family and Marriage Review,* in press.

Kleinman, A. M. "Depression, Somatization, and the 'New Cross-Cultural Psychiatry.'" *Social Science and Medicine,* 1977, *11,* 3-10.

Kleinman, A. M. *Patients and Healers in the Context of Culture.* Berkeley: University of California Press, 1979.

Kleinman, A. M., and Sung, L. H. "Why Do Indigenous Practitioners Successfully Heal?" *Social Science and Medicine,* 1979, *13B,* 7-26.

Klopf, D. W., and Cambra, R. E. "Communication Apprehension Among College Students in America, Australia, Japan, and Korea." *Journal of Psychology,* 1979, *102,* 27-31.

Kluckhohn, C., and Murray, H. A. "Personality Formation: The Determinants." In C. Kluckhohn (Ed.), *Personality in Nature, Society and Culture.* New York: Knopf, 1956.

Korchin, S. J. *Modern Clinical Psychology.* New York: Basic Books, 1976.

Korchin, S. J. "Clinical Psychology and Minority Problems." *American Psychologist,* 1980, *35,* 262-269.

Koseki, L. K. "Civil Rights and Affirmative Action: Issues, Dilemmas, and Alternatives." In U. S. Commission on Civil Rights (Ed.), *Civil Rights Issues of Asian and Pacific Americans: Myths and Realities.* Washington, D.C.: U.S. Government Printing Office, 1980.

Kramer, B. M. "Community Mental Health in a Dual Society."

In S. Sue and T. Moore (Eds.), *The Pluralistic Society: A Community Mental Health Perspective.* New York: Human Sciences Press, 1982.

Kramer, M., Rosen, B. M., and Willis, E. M. "Definitions and Distributions of Mental Disorders in a Racist Society." In C. V. Willie, B. M. Kramer, and B. S. Brown (Eds.), *Racism and Mental Health: Essays.* Pittsburgh: University of Pittsburgh Press, 1973.

Kriger, S. F., and Kroes, W. H. "Child-Rearing Attitudes of Chinese, Jewish, and Protestant Mothers." *Journal of Social Psychology,* 1972, *86,* 205-210.

Kroeber, A., and Kluckhohn, C. *Culture.* Cambridge, Mass.: Peabody Museum, Harvard University, 1952.

Kubany, E. S., Gallimore, R., and Buell, J. "The Effects of Extrinsic Factors on Achievement-Oriented Behavior: A Non-Western Case." *Journal of Cross-Cultural Psychology,* 1970, *1,* 77-84.

Kuo, W. "Theories of Migration and Mental Health: An Empirical Testing on Chinese Americans." *Social Science and Medicine,* 1976, *10,* 297-306.

Kuramoto, F. H. "Lessons Learned in the Federal Funding Game." *Social Casework,* 1976, *57,* 208-218.

Kurokawa, M. "Acculturation and Childhood Accidents Among Chinese and Japanese Americans." *Genetic Psychology Monographs,* 1969, *79,* 89-159.

Lee, E. "Mental Health Services for the Asian Americans: Problems and Alternatives." In U.S. Commission on Civil Rights (Ed.), *Civil Rights Issues of Asian and Pacific Americans: Myths and Realities.* Washington, D.C.: U.S. Government Printing Office, 1980.

Lim, D. T. "Some Unmeltable Issues in Asian American Mental Health." Paper presented at a conference on Asian American mental health, Canada College, Redwood City, Calif., Oct. 1977.

Lin, T. Y., and others. "Ethnicity and Patterns of Help-Seeking." *Culture, Medicine, and Psychiatry,* 1978, *2,* 3-13.

Liu, W. T. "Community Research and the Asian American Mental Health Research Center." In A. K. Murata and J. Salvador-Burris (Eds.), *Issues in Community Research: Asian American Perspectives.* Chicago: Pacific/Asian Mental Health Research Center, 1980.

Liu, W. T., and Murata, A. K. "Vietnamese in America. Part Four: Life in the Refugee Camps." *Bridge,* 1978, *6,* 44-49.

Long, P. B. "The Issue of Family Reunification Facing Indochinese Refugees in the U.S." In U.S. Commission of Civil Rights (Ed.), *Civil Rights Issues of Asian and Pacific Americans: Myths and Realities.* Washington, D.C.: U.S. Government Printing Office, 1980.

Loo, C., and Yu, C. Y. "Chinatown: Recording Reality, Destroying Myths." Paper presented at a symposium at the American Psychological Association convention, Montreal, Sept. 1980.

Lorr, M., and Vestre, N. D. *Psychotic Inpatient Profile Manual.* Los Angeles: Western Psychological Services, 1968.

Lu, F. G. "The Asian and Pacific American In-Patient Psychiatric Program at San Francisco General Hospital." Paper presented at the conference on Innovations in the Mental Health Care of Asian Americans, New York, June 1981.

Luce, P. H. "The Identification Crisis of Pacific Americans and Its Implications for Educational Opportunities." In U.S. Commission on Civil Rights (Ed.), *Civil Rights Issues of Asian and Pacific Americans: Myths and Realities.* Washington, D.C.: U.S. Government Printing Office, 1980.

Lum, R. "Issues in the Study of Asian American Communities." Paper presented at meeting of the Western Psychological Association, San Francisco, April 1974.

Lyman, S. M. *Chinese Americans.* New York: Random House, 1974.

Lyman, S. M. "Chinese Secret Societies in the Occident: Notes and Suggestions for Research in the Sociology of Secrecy." In S. M. Lyman (Ed.), *The Asian in North America.* Santa Barbara, Calif.: ABC-Clio, 1977.

McGrath, J. E. "Social Science, Social Action, and the *Journal of Social Issues." Journal of Social Issues,* 1980, *36,* 109-124.

Markoff, R. A., and Bond, J. R. "The Samoans of Hawaii." In

W. S. Tseng, J. F. McDermott, and T. W. Maretzki (Eds.), *People and Cultures in Hawaii.* Honolulu: University Press of Hawaii, 1974.

Marsella, A. J., Kinzie, D., and Gordon, P. "Ethnic Variations in the Expression of Depression." *Journal of Cross-Cultural Psychology,* 1973, *4,* 435-458.

Masuda, M., Matsumoto, G. M., and Meredith, G. M. "Ethnic Identity in Three Generations of Japanese-Americans." *Journal of Social Psychology,* 1970, *81,* 199-207.

Matsumoto, G. M., Meredith, G. M., and Masuda, M. "Ethnic Identity: Honolulu and Seattle Japanese Americans." *Journal of Cross-Cultural Psychology,* 1970, *1,* 63-76.

Maykovich, M. "White-Yellow Stereotypes: An Empirical Study." *Pacific Sociological Review,* 1971, *14,* 447-467.

Maykovich, M. "Reciprocity in Racial Stereotypes: White, Black, and Yellow." *American Journal of Sociology,* 1972, *77,* 876-897.

Meade, R. D. "Leadership Studies of Chinese and Chinese-Americans." *Journal of Cross-Cultural Psychology,* 1970, *1,* 325-332.

Mercer, J. R. "Institutionalized Anglocentrism: Labeling Mental Retardates in the Public Schools." In P. Orleans and W. R. Ellis (Eds.), *Race, Change, and Urban Society.* Beverly Hills, Calif.: Sage, 1971.

Meredith, G. M. "Amae and Acculturation Among Japanese American College Students in Hawaii." *Journal of Social Psychology,* 1966, *70,* 171-180.

Meredith, G. M. "Sex Temperament Among Japanese-American College Students in Hawaii." *Journal of Social Psychology,* 1969, *77,* 149-156.

Meredith, G. M., and Meredith, C. W. "Acculturation and Personality Among Japanese-American College Students in Hawaii." *Journal of Social Psychology,* 1966, *68,* 175-182.

Miyamoto, F. "Issues in Community Research." In A. K. Murata and J. Salvador-Burris (Eds.), *Issues in Community Research: Asian American Perspectives.* Chicago: Pacific/Asian Mental Health Research Center, 1980.

Mizokawa, D. T., and Morishima, J. K. "The Education for, by, and of Asian/Pacific Americans." Part I. *Research Review of Equal Education,* 1979, *3,* 1-33.

Montero, D. "Research Among Racial and Cultural Minorities." *Journal of Social Issues,* 1977, *33,* 1-10.

Morales, R. F. *Makibaka: The Filipino American Struggle.* Darby, Mont.: Mountain View, 1974.

Morishima, J. K. "Early History, 1850-1965: The Meeting of the Twain." In J. K. Morishima (Ed.), *Report on the Asian American Assessment Colloquy.* Washington, D.C.: Child Development Associate Consortium, 1975.

Morishima, J. K. "The Asian American Experience: 1850-1975." *Journal of the Society of Ethnic and Special Studies,* 1978, *2,* 8-10.

Morishima, J. K. "Asian American Racial Mixes: Attitudes, Self-Concept, and Academic Performance." Paper presented at Western Psychological Association convention, Honolulu, April 1980.

Morishima, J. K., and Mizokawa, D. T. "The Education for, by, and of Asian/Pacific Americans." Part II. *Research Review of Equal Education,* 1979, *4,* 1-39.

Morishima, J. K., and others. *Handbook of Asian American/ Pacific Islander Mental Health.* Vol. 1. Washington, D.C.: U.S. Government Printing Office, 1979.

Moritsugu, J., Foerster, L., and Morishima, J. K. "Eurasians: A Pilot Study." Paper presented at the Western Psychological Association convention, San Francisco, 1978.

Multicultural Drug Abuse Prevention Resource Center. *First National Asian American Conference on Drug Abuse Prevention.* Los Angeles: Multicultural Resource Center, 1976.

Munoz, F. U. "Pacific Islanders: Life Patterns in a New Land." In R. Endo, S. Sue, and N. N. Wagner (Eds.), *Asian Americans: Social and Psychological Perspectives.* Palo Alto, Calif.: Science and Behavior Books, 1980.

Murase, K. "State and Local Public Policy Issues in Delivering Mental Health and Related Services to Asian and Pacific Americans." In U.S. Commission on Civil Rights (Ed.), *Civil Rights Issues of Asian and Pacific Americans: Myths and Realities.* Washington, D.C.: U.S. Government Printing Office, 1980.

Nakagawa, B., and Watanabe, R. *A Study of the Use of Drugs Among the Asian American Youth of Seattle.* Seattle: Demonstration Project of Asian Americans, 1973.

Ochberg, F. M., and Brown, B. S. "Key Issues in Developing a National Minority Mental Health Program at NIMH." In C. V. Willie, B. M. Kramer, and B. S. Brown (Eds.), *Racism and Mental Health: Essays.* Pittsburgh: University of Pittsburgh Press, 1973.

Ogawa, D. M. *From Japs to Japanese: The Evolution of Japanese-American Stereotypes.* Berkeley: McCutchan, 1971.

Ogawa, D. M. *Jan Ken Po: The World of Hawaii's Japanese Americans.* Honolulu: Obun, 1973.

Oka, B. J., Cambra, R. E., and Klopf, D. W. "Reducing Apprehension About Communication." *Psychological Reports,* 1979, *44,* 430.

Olmedo, E. L. "Acculturation: A Psychometric Perspective." *American Psychologist,* 1979, *34,* 1061-1070.

Opler, M. K. *Culture and Social Psychiatry.* New York: Lieber-Atherton, 1967.

Osako, M. M. "Intergenerational Relations as an Aspect of Assimilation: The Case of Japanese Americans." *Sociological Inquiry,* 1976, *46,* 67-72.

Owan, T. "Asian Americans: A Case of Benighted Neglect." Paper presented at meeting of the National Conference of Social Welfare, San Francisco, May 1975.

Padilla, A. M., Ruiz, R. A., and Alvarez, R. "Community Mental Health Services for the Spanish-Speaking/Surnamed Population." *American Psychologist,* 1975, *30,* 892-905.

Paik, I. "That Oriental Feeling." In A. Tachiki and others (Eds.), *Roots: An Asian American Reader.* Los Angeles: Continental Graphics, 1971.

Pang, V. O. "The Self-Concept of Japanese American and White American Children in the Fourth Through Sixth Grade as Measured by a Modified Piers-Harris Children's Self Concept Scale." Unpublished doctoral dissertation, University of Washington, 1981.

Park, P. "A New Model for Community Action Research." In A. K. Murata and J. Salvador-Burris (Eds.), *Issues in Commu-*

nity Research: Asian American Perspectives. Chicago: Pacific/
Asian Mental Health Research Center, 1980.

Pedersen, P. B., Lonner, W. J., and Draguns, J. G. (Eds.). *Counseling Across Cultures.* Honolulu: University Press of Hawaii, 1976.

Peralta, V. "Community Services—State and Local Policy." In U.S. Commission on Civil Rights (Ed.), *Civil Rights Issues of Asian and Pacific Americans: Myths and Realities.* Washington, D.C.: U.S. Government Printing Office, 1980.

Peralta, V., and Horikawa, H. *Needs and Potentialities Assessment of Asian American Elderly in Greater Philadelphia.* Report No. 3. Chicago: Asian American Mental Health Research Center, 1978.

Petersen, W. "Chinese Americans and Japanese Americans." In T. Sowell (Ed.), *Essays and Data on American Ethnic Groups.* Washington, D.C.: Urban Institute, 1978.

Pian, C. "Consultation Focus: Identification of Issues." In U.S. Commission on Civil Rights (Ed.), *Civil Rights Issues of Asian and Pacific Americans: Myths and Realities.* Washington, D.C.: U.S. Government Printing Office, 1980.

Ponce, D. E. "The Filipinos of Hawaii." In W. S. Tseng, J. F. McDermott, and T. W. Maretzki (Eds.), *People and Cultures in Hawaii.* Honolulu: University Press of Hawaii, 1974.

Ponce, D. E. "Intercultural Perspectives on Mate Selection." In W. S. Tseng, J. F. McDermott, and T. W. Maretzki (Eds.), *Adjustment in Intercultural Marriage.* Honolulu: University Press of Hawaii, 1977.

President's Commission on Mental Health. *Report to the President.* 4 Vols. Washington, D.C.: U.S. Government Printing Office, 1978.

Prizzia, R., and Villanueva-King, O. *Central Oahu Community Mental Health Needs Assessment Survey.* Part III: *A Survey of the General Population.* Honolulu: Management Planning and Administration Consultants, 1977.

Quinsaat, J. "Introduction." In E. Gee (Ed.), *Counterpoint: Perspectives on Asian America.* Los Angeles: Asian American Studies Center, 1977.

Rahe, R. H., and others. "Psychiatric Consultation in a Vietnamese Refugee Camp." *American Journal of Psychiatry*, 1978, *135*, 185-190.

Rappaport, J. *Community Psychology: Values, Research, Action*. New York: Holt, Rinehart and Winston, 1977.

Rappaport, J. "In Praise of Paradox: A Social Policy of Empowerment over Prevention." *American Journal of Community Psychology*, 1981, *9*, 1-25.

Rogers, C. R., and Skinner, B. F. "Some Issues Concerning the Control of Human Behavior." *Science*, 1956, *124*, 1057-1066.

Sarason, S. B. "Community Psychology and the Anarchist Insight." *American Journal of Community Psychology*, 1976, *4*, 256-261.

Sata, L. S., and Lin, K. M. *Culturally Relevant Training for Asian American Psychiatrists*. Washington, D.C.: American Psychiatric Association, 1977.

Scott, W. A. "Research Definitions of Mental Health and Mental Illness." *Psychological Bulletin*, 1958, *55*, 29-45.

Seligman, M. P. *Helplessness: On Depression, Development and Death*. San Francisco: W. H. Freeman, 1975.

Shon, S. "The Delivery of Mental Health Services to Asian and Pacific Americans." In U.S. Commission on Civil Rights (Ed.), *Civil Rights Issues of Asian and Pacific Americans: Myths and Realities*. Washington, D.C.: U.S. Government Printing Office, 1980a.

Shon, S. "Some Aspects of Psychotherapy with Asian and Pacific People." Paper presented at the Langley Porter annual faculty alumni conference, San Francisco, April 1980b.

Shu, R., and Satele, A. S. *The Samoan Community in Southern California: Conditions and Needs*. Chicago: Asian American Mental Health Research Center, 1977.

Sigall, H., and Page, R. "Current Stereotypes: A Little Fading, a Little Faking." *Journal of Personality and Social Psychology*, 1971, *18*, 247-255.

Skinner, B. F. *Beyond Freedom and Dignity*. New York: Knopf, 1971.

Sollenberger, R. T. "Chinese American Child-Rearing Practices and Juvenile Delinquency." *Journal of Social Psychology*, 1968, *74*, 13-23.

Sommers, V. S. "Identity Conflict and Acculturation Problems in Oriental Americans." *American Journal of Orthopsychiatry,* 1960, *30,* 637-644.

Special Services for Groups. *Pacific/Asian Elderly Research Project: Final Report.* Los Angeles: Special Services for Groups, 1978. (Mimeographed.)

State of Hawaii. *Statistical Report of the Department of Health.* Honolulu: Department of Health, 1970, 1972.

State of Hawaii. *Report of the Department of Planning and Economic Development.* Honolulu: Department of Planning, 1978.

Stevens, A. J. "The Acquisition of Participatory Norms: The Case of Japanese- and Mexican-American Children in a Suburban Environment." *Western Political Quarterly,* 1975, *28,* 281-295.

Steward, M., and Steward, D. "The Observation of Anglo-, Mexican-, and Chinese-American Mothers Teaching Their Young Sons." *Child Development,* 1973, *44,* 329-337.

Sue, D. W. *Counseling the Culturally Different: Theory and Practice.* New York: Wiley, 1981.

Sue, D. W., and Kirk, B. A. "Psychological Characteristics of Chinese American Students." *Journal of Counseling Psychology,* 1972, *19,* 471-478.

Sue, D. W., and Kirk, B. A. "Differential Characteristics of Japanese-American and Chinese-American College Students." *Journal of Counseling Psychology,* 1973, *20,* 142-148.

Sue, D. W., and Kirk, B. A. "Asian Americans: Use of Counseling and Psychiatric Services on a College Campus." *Journal of Counseling Psychology,* 1975, *22,* 84-86.

Sue, D. W., and Sue, S. "Ethnic Minorities: Resistance to Being Researched." *Professional Psychology,* 1972, *3,* 11-17.

Sue, S. "Personality and Mental Health: A Clarification." *Amerasia Journal,* 1974, *2,* 173-177.

Sue, S. "Community Mental Health Services to Minority Groups: Some Optimism, Some Pessimism." *American Psychologist,* 1977a, *32,* 616-624.

Sue, S. "Psychological Theory and Implications for Asian Americans." *Personnel and Guidance Journal,* 1977b, *55,* 381-389.

Sue, S. "Challenge to Human Service Providers." Keynote address at a conference on Decade of Change: A Challenge to Human Service Providers, University of California, Berkeley, April 1980.

Sue, S. "Ethnic Minority Issues in Psychology: Something Old, Something New." Invited address presented at meeting of the Western Psychological Association, Los Angeles, April 1981a.

Sue, S. "Mental Health Treatment Issues for Asian Americans." Paper presented at meeting of the Western Psychological Association, Los Angeles, April 1981b.

Sue, S., and Chin, R. "Chinese American Children: Psychosocial Development and Mental Health." In G. Powell, A. Morales, and J. Yamamoto (Eds.), *The Psychosocial Development of Minority Group Children.* New York: Brunner/Mazel, 1982.

Sue, S., Ito, J., and Bradshaw, C. "Ethnic Minority Research: Trends and Directions." In E. E. Jones and S. J. Korchin (Eds.), *Minority Mental Health.* New York: Praeger, 1982.

Sue, S., and Kitano, H. H. L. "Stereotypes as a Measure of Success." *Journal of Social Issues,* 1973, *29,* 83-98.

Sue, S., and McKinney, H. "Asian-Americans in the Community Mental Health Care System." *American Journal of Orthopsychiatry,* 1975, *45,* 111-118.

Sue, S., and Sue, D. W. "Chinese American Personality and Mental Health." *Amerasia Journal,* 1971, *1,* 36-49.

Sue, S., and Sue, D. W. "Chinese American Personality and Mental Health: A Reply to Tong's Criticisms." *Amerasia Journal,* 1972, *1,* 60-65.

Sue, S., and Sue, D. W. "MMPI Comparisons Between Asian-American and Non-Asian Students Utilizing a Student Health Psychiatric Clinic." *Journal of Counseling Psychology,* 1974, *21,* 423-427.

Sue, S., Sue, D. W., and Sue, D. "Asian Americans as a Minority Group." *American Psychologist,* 1975, *30,* 906-910.

Sue, S., Zane, N., and Ito, J. "Alcohol Drinking Patterns Among Asian and Caucasian Americans." *Journal of Cross-Cultural Psychology,* 1979, *10,* 41-56.

Sue, S., and others. "Conceptions of Mental Illness Among

Asian- and Caucasian-American Students." *Psychological Reports,* 1976, *38,* 703-708.

Sung, B. L. *The Story of the Chinese in America.* New York: Macmillan, 1967.

Sung, B. L. *Transplanted Chinese Children.* Report to the Administration for Children, Youth and Families. Washington, D.C.: Department of Health, Education and Welfare, 1979.

Surh, J. "Asian American Identity and Politics." *Amerasia Journal,* 1974, *2,* 158-172.

Suzuki, B. H. "Education and the Socialization of Asian Americans: A Revisionist Analysis of the 'Model Minority' Thesis." *Amerasia Journal,* 1977, *4,* 23-52.

Takagi, P. "The Myth of 'Assimilation in American Life.' " *Amerasia Journal,* 1973, *2,* 149-158.

Tanaka, R. "I Hate My Wife for Her Flat Yellow Face." In A. Tachiki and others (Eds.), *Roots: An Asian American Reader.* Los Angeles: Continental Graphics, 1971.

Thein, T. M. "Health Issues Affecting Asian/Pacific American Women." In U.S. Commission on Civil Rights (Ed.), *Civil Rights Issues of Asian and Pacific Americans: Myths and Realities.* Washington, D.C.: U.S. Government Printing Office, 1980.

Thomas, A., and Sillen, A. *Racism and Psychiatry.* New York: Brunner/Mazel, 1972.

Tinker, J. N. "Intermarriage and Ethnic Boundaries: The Japanese American Case." *Journal of Social Issues,* 1973, *29,* 49-66.

Tom, S. "Mental Health in the Chinese Community of San Francisco." Unpublished paper, 1968.

Tong, B. R. "The Ghetto of the Mind: Notes on the Historical Psychology of Chinese-America." *Amerasia Journal,* 1971, *1,* 1-31.

Tong, B. R. "Reply to Sues." *Amerasia Journal,* 1972a, *1,* 65-67.

Tong, B. R. "Response to Abbott." *Amerasia Journal,* 1972b, *1,* 74-75.

Tong, B. R. "Letter to the Editor." *Amerasia Journal,* 1973, *2,* 182.

Tong, B. R. "A Living Death Defended as a Legacy of a Superior Culture." *Amerasia Journal,* 1974, *2,* 178-202.

Triandis, H. C. *The Analysis of Subjective Culture*. New York: Wiley, 1972.

Trimble, J. E. "Value Differences Among American Indians: Concerns for the Concerned Counselor." In P. B. Pedersen, W. J. Lonner, and J. G. Draguns (Eds.), *Counseling Across Cultures*. Honolulu: University Press of Hawaii, 1976.

Tsai, M., Teng, L. N., and Sue, S. "Mental Status of Chinese in the United States." In A. Kleinman and T. Y. Lin (Eds.), *Normal and Deviant Behavior in Chinese Culture*. Hingham, Mass.: Reidel, 1980.

Tseng, W. S., and Char, W. F. "The Chinese of Hawaii." In W. S. Tseng, J. F. McDermott, and T. W. Maretzki (Eds.), *People and Cultures in Hawaii*. Honolulu: University Press of Hawaii, 1974.

U.S. Commission on Civil Rights (Ed.). *Civil Rights Issues of Asian and Pacific Americans: Myths and Realities*. Washington, D.C.: U.S. Government Printing Office, 1980.

U.S. Comptroller General. *The Indochinese Exodus: A Humanitarian Dilemma*. Washington, D.C.: U.S. Government Printing Office, 1979.

Urban Associates. *A Study of Selected Socio-Economic Characteristics of Ethnic Minorities Based on the 1970 Census*. Vol. 2: *Asian Americans*. Washington, D.C.: U.S. Government Printing Office, 1974.

Vontress, C. E. *Counseling Negroes*. Boston: Houghton Mifflin, 1971.

Wang, L., and Louie, W. "The Chinatown Aftercare Program: A Report on a Selected Group of Chinese Patients and Their State Hospital Experience." Unpublished paper, 1979.

Weiss, J. A., and Weiss, M. S. "Social Scientists and Decision Makers Look at the Usefulness of Mental Health Research." *American Psychologist*, 1981, *36*, 837-847.

Weiss, M. S. "Selective Acculturation and the Dating Process: The Pattern of Chinese-Caucasian Interracial Dating." *Journal of Marriage and the Family*, 1970, *32*, 273-278.

Weiss, M. S. *Valley City: A Chinese Community in America*. Cambridge, Mass.: Schenkman, 1974.

Williams, R. L. "The BITCH-100: A Culture-Specific Test." *Journal of Afro-American Issues*, 1975, *3*, 103-116.

Wolff, P. H. "Ethnic Differences in Alcohol Sensitivity." *Science,* 1972, *175,* 449-450.

Wolkon, G. H., and Yamamoto, J. "Medical Student Attitudes About Quality Care and Training of Minority Persons." *Journal of the National Medical Association,* 1978, *70,* 185-188.

Wong, H. Z. "Community Mental Health Services and Manpower and Training Concerns of Asian Americans." Mimeograph of testimony presented before the President's Commission on Mental Health, San Francisco, March 1977.

Wong, H. Z. "Contextual Factors for the Development of the National Asian American Psychology Training Center." *Journal of Community Psychology,* 1981, *9,* 289-292.

Wong, J. "Indochinese Refugees: The Mental Health Perspectives." In U.S. Commission on Civil Rights (Ed.), *Civil Rights Issues of Asian and Pacific Americans: Myths and Realities.* Washington, D.C.: U.S. Government Printing Office, 1980.

Wu, D. Y. H. "Emotion and Mental Health in Traditional Chinese Medicine." Paper presented at conference on Cultural Conceptions of Mental Health and Therapy, Honolulu, June 1980.

Wu, I. H., and Windle, C. "Ethnic Specificity in the Relationship of Minority Use and Staffing of Community Mental Health Centers." *Community Mental Health Journal,* 1980, *16,* 156-168.

Yamamoto, J., James, Q. C., and Palley, N. "Cultural Problems in Psychiatric Therapy." *Archives of General Psychiatry,* 1968, *19,* 45-49.

Yamamoto, J., and Satele, A. "Samoans in California." *Psychiatric Journal of the University of Ottawa,* 1979, *4,* 349-352.

Yamamoto, J., and Wagatsuma, H. "The Japanese and Japanese Americans." *Journal of Operational Psychiatry,* 1980, *11,* 120-135.

Yee, T. "Chinese American Conceptualization of Physical and Mental Well-Being." *Dissertation Abstracts International,* 1980, *41,* No. 2, Order No. 8016652.

Young, N. F. "Changes in Values and Strategies Among Chinese in Hawaii." *Sociology and Social Research,* 1972a, *56,* 228-241.

Young, N. F. "Independence Training from a Cross-Cultural Perspective." *American Anthropologist,* 1972b, *74,* 629-638.

Zubin, J., and Spring, B. "Vulnerability—A New View of Schizophrenia." *Journal of Abnormal Psychology,* 1977, *86,* 103-126.

Index

Abasement, as personality trait, 99
Abbott, E., 66, 97
Abbott, K. A., 66, 91, 101
Acculturation: and assimilation, 107, 163; defined, 100; by females, 113-114; and intergroup marriage, 110
Achievement motivation, as personality trait, 100
Affective states: primary, 50-51; secondary, 50-51
Affirmative action, 8, 9
Aggression: in classroom management, 136-138; and personality, 99
Albee, G., 90
Alcantara, R. R., 65
Alcohol: consumption of, 61-63; psychological reactions to, 11
Allport, G. W., 110
Alternative resources, availability of, 28-30
Alvarez, R., 21
Ambiguity, in personality research, 99
Antimiscegenation law, 112-113
Antimony: and Asian and Pacific American research issues, 184-186; defined, 183
Anti-social personality, 16

Anxiety, 37. *See also* Speech anxiety
Arkoff, A., 33, 99, 100, 106, 111, 113, 162
Arthur, R. J., 53-54
Asian American: and alcohol, 62-63; elderly, 57-59; numbers of, 2-3; personality, 93-105; and psychiatric diagnosis, 50; stereotype, 120. *See also* specific ethnic group
Asian American Psychiatrists, Task Force on, 132
Asian American Psychological Association, 132
Asian and Pacific American Subpanel, 4, 133
Asian Community Mental Health Services, 148, 149
Asian Counseling and Referral Service, 31, 149
Asian/Pacific Counseling and Treatment Center, 149
"Asian Women As Leaders," 105
Assertiveness, as personality trait, 99
Assimilation: defined, 100; and interracial marriage, 107, 110, 112; issues of, 163-164; as model, 7
Atkinson, D. R., 140

213